40 *Unforgettable* Dates with Your Mate

# 40 *unforgettable* dates with your mate

## DR. GARY & BARBARA ROSBERG
*with Tom and Linda Taylor*

TYNDALE HOUSE PUBLISHERS, INC. I CAROL STREAM, ILLINOIS

Visit Tyndale's exciting Web site at www.tyndale.com

*TYNDALE* and Tyndale's quill logo are registered trademarks of Tyndale House Publishers, Inc.

*40 Unforgettable Dates with Your Mate*

Published in association with the literary agency of Alive Communications, Inc., 7680 Goddard Street, Suite 200, Colorado Springs, CO 80920.

Some discussion questions in this book are adapted from *We're Finally Alone—Now What Do We Do?* by Greg Johnson (Tyndale House, 1996). Used by permission.

Three dates in chapter 11 are adapted from the game "Simply Romantic Nights" (FamilyLife, 2000) by Dennis and Barbara Rainey, Gary and Barbara Rosberg, and others. To obtain the game, contact FamilyLife Ministries at www.familylife.com or (888)FL-TODAY.

Designed by Kelly Bennema

Edited by Lynn Vanderzalm

The names and some of the details in the illustrations used in this book have been changed to protect the privacy of the people who shared their stories with us.

**Library of Congress Cataloging-in-Publication Data**

Rosberg, Gary, date.
    40 unforgettable dates with your mate / Gary and Barbara Rosberg, with Tom and Linda Taylor.
        p.   cm.
title: Forty unforgettable dates with your mate.
    ISBN-13: 978-0-8423-6106-4 (sc)
    ISBN-10: 0-8423-6106-5 (sc)
    1. Marriage. 2. Dating (Social customs) 3. Marriage—Religious aspects—Christianity.   I. Title:
Forty unforgettabe dates with your mate.   II. Rosberg, Barbara.   III. Taylor, Tom.   IV. Taylor,
Linda.   V. Title.
HQ734 .R755 2002
306.81—dc21                                                                              2002001873

Printed in the United States of America

11   10   09   08   07
8    7    6    5    4

To our parents
*Thank you for loving each other for a lifetime.*
*It is the greatest gift you gave to your children.*

To Sarah and Scott
*Drink this up, and celebrate your marriage.*
*We are crazy about you two!*

To Missy
*Your passion for Jesus inspires us daily.*
*Guard your heart, honey. You are terrific!*

To Mason, our grandson
*Someday this will make sense to you,*
*but right now let's get you through diapers!*

*We love you all.*

# contents

## Part 3: A Wife Plans Dates for Her Husband

# acknowledgments

Our passion is writing books that make a difference:
- For you and your marriage;
- For your family;
- For your relationships;
- And primarily for the glory of God.

In the past we have tackled resolving conflict and granting forgiveness (Dr. Rosberg's Do-It-Yourself Relationship Mender), maintaining moral purity (Guard Your Heart), strengthening marital communication (Improving Communication in Your Marriage), and learning and seeking to meet your spouse's love needs (The Five Love Needs of Men and Women). Soon we will be launching a multiyear campaign to challenge the church, culture, and you to divorce-proof America's marriages—for the sake of the next generation.

Yet in the midst of writing these challenging and life-changing books, we concluded that we wanted to come up for air with you, our readers, and equip you to celebrate "dating your mate." Over the last several years we have done a series of conferences entitled "Date with a Purpose" and wanted to put in writing our ideas to expand that concept from a conference to a book that could strengthen marriages and relationships beyond our conferences. Hence the idea for this book. We wanted to give you ideas and a strategy to zero in on the needs of your mate and celebrate the love of your life. And we didn't do it alone.

This book is the idea of our agent, Greg Johnson, from Alive Communications. He also has contributed to the book with discussion questions from a book he wrote several years ago.

Thank you, Greg, for the vision and, again, for introducing us to Ron Beers and Tyndale House Publishers. We are forever grateful.

Speaking of Tyndale House, we want to thank you for teaming up with us to make a difference in marriages in America and beyond. Ron Beers, Ken Petersen, and Team Tyndale are the best in the publishing industry. Bar none. Your integrity, passion, and commitment to excellence set the bar in Christian publishing. In addition, we love you all as friends. We want to honor God and you in all of our books and are thrilled to team with you to minister to our readers. Our special thanks, again, to Lynn Vanderzalm for sweetening this manuscript. She is not only an extraordinary wordsmith and editor but a dear friend as well. Thanks also to Kelly Bennema for a great cover design.

It is our joy to welcome Tom and Linda Taylor to our publishing team for this book. This gracious couple developed our "date with a purpose" idea and helped us craft the manuscript into what you see today. It was a delight to have a couple who, like us, celebrate marriage and the importance of dating your mate. Thank you for your passion and investment in this book. We pray couples will reach new levels of celebration because of your efforts.

We not only celebrate our publishing team, but we also want to honor our "home team." To the entire ministry team at America's Family Coaches: Bless you. Your commitment to serving the Lord and us equips us to keep our passion for publishing life-changing and equipping books a priority. We couldn't do what we do if you didn't so effectively help us with our daily radio programs, national conferences, and the weekly CrossTrainers men's ministry. We appreciate you all more than you know.

And finally, thanks to the best family on earth. We are so thankful to our kids for being the real deal and living lives that glorify Christ in public and, more important, in private. What an honor to be your mom and dad. Sarah and Scott, you are such a delight. We pray this book encourages you in your marriage to celebrate each other for life. Missy, your passion for Jesus inspires us beyond your wildest imagination. Stay the course, honey. And Mason, our new grandson, someday you will read this as you learn to date your wife. Honor her, cherish her, and love her unconditionally, Grandson. It's worked for your grandparents, and we believe it will work for you! We deeply love you.

*Gary and Barb Rosberg*

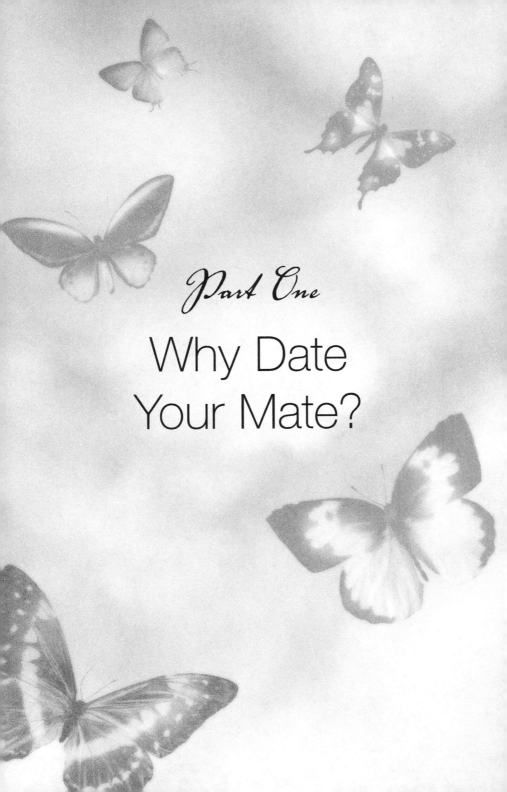

*Part One*

# Why Date Your Mate?

*~ Chapter One ~*

# Sweaty Palms and Butterflies—Going on a Date!

You remember what it was like, don't you—way back when. Back when you were in high school or college and "dating" was what you did as a social activity and as a way to discover that "special person." Back when your inexperience and immaturity made for all kinds of difficulty in going through the dating rituals.

Guys, remember how it was? You spotted that girl and were keeping an eye on her for some time. You watched her at school, in class, in other activities. You thought her hair and clothes were really nice; she had a pretty face; she seemed friendly. Your radar was tuned to her frequency. When she entered a room, you just *knew* it and would turn to notice, and watch. You began to move in a bit closer. Sat at the same table. Tried for a bit of conversation. You battled with all the inner doubts and questions. Would she even give you the time of day? Would she think you were a geek? Did you look (and smell) all right? Then you decided to ask her out. Your palms sweat. How were you going to make sure she would say yes? Or, if she said no, how would you make sure it caused minimal damage to your fragile self-esteem?

In the meantime, over at another table, another young lady had her radar set on *your* frequency. She began watching you—at lunch, at the games, in the classroom, with your friends. She moved in closer—dying for a look from you, a brief exchange of words with you so that she could say she made contact. She was hoping you would ask her out!

Women, do you remember being in one of those positions? Perhaps you never saw the guy coming—and suddenly he was right in front of you, sweaty palms and all. Maybe he wasn't your type, so you said no and walked away, leaving a shattered self-esteem littered over the school hallway. Maybe he seemed interesting, and you said yes—with trepidation. Or maybe that dreamboat actually *did* make his way down the hall and ask you out. In your stomach you felt butterflies that threatened to actually take you off the ground in flight with them when you said yes to a *date* with the man of your dreams!

And we haven't even started talking about the night of the date yet! You thought your palms were sweating or your stomach had no more room for butterflies *before*. But remember what happened on those dates? We do.

I can still remember the first time I saw Barb. And I still get light-headed with the memory. I was standing at the front door of her sorority at Drake University to recruit volunteers for a project (someone had to do it), and she had just run up the walk. I recall thinking, *Where did she come from?* I thought I knew every pretty student on campus. Little did I know she had recently transferred into Drake.

In one phrase, my reaction to her was, *Yippie kae yae yay!* She knocked me out!

A few days later we were set up on a blind date, and as they say, "the rest is history." We spent our first few dates going to college basketball games and the pancake house, and we talked endless hours on the phone. We courted at the mall where Barb sold jewelry and china in a fine shop and where I was a longhaired shoe salesman in a hip clothing store. I was attracted to her outer beauty (and still am), then her personality and character. Ultimately I was drawn to her spiritual life as she, along with a Campus Crusade for Christ guy, led me to Christ. I'll let Barb tell you about the first time I asked her out . . . without the revisionist history side.

~ ~ ~

It was a cold February night, and I was out of breath when I arrived at the front door of my sorority house, late—again— for a house meeting. And there he stood.

"I'm here to speak to the women and recruit volunteers for a juvenile delinquency project," he said nervously.

My eyes locked on the most handsome man I had ever seen. His long brown hair framed magnificent warm eyes that somehow pulled me in. For a moment I got light-headed.

"Come on in!" I responded.

The meeting was already in session. I nestled into the group of young women on the floor, and the guy began talking to the group.

"Pssst, do you know who that is?" My friend said and nudged me. "That's Gary Rosberg, the guy we've been dying to set you up with!"

My heart beat a little faster, and I felt flushed. My sorority sisters had been talking to me for months about a guy on campus, but I wasn't exactly interested. Until then he was just a name without a face.

That night the face became a reality, and I would never forget it. I was enchanted by his good looks.

But it was more than his looks. Gary was commanding as a speaker. He was funny, informative, and deliberate. Glancing around the room, I saw a group of women mesmerized as he expressed his passion for kids.

I didn't sign up that night as a volunteer, but looking back, it's clear that I got recruited all right. I was captivated by this man's charisma.

A week later my friends cajoled me into "just meeting him."

So in the middle of a social gathering between the Phi Delt's and Alpha Phi's, in the center of a human circle, Gary and I were pushed to be introduced. It was very awkward, so we took off and headed to opposite ends of the room. But I wasn't stupid, so when everyone was distracted, I moseyed through the rooms to find Gary again. And I did.

He seemed a lot more at ease. We talked for quite a while, mostly about kids.

After the gathering I said to my friends, "Wow. He is sharp." And that was the end of that.

Until he called me the next day.

We talked for three hours. He was charming, and I was fascinated by his stories (and I still am). Then toward the end of the conversation he asked me out for a date on the weekend.

*Oh no,* I thought. I wasn't prepared for him to ask me out. I opened my mouth and blurted out, "I'm sorry, I can't Friday night. I need to break up with someone I've been dating for a while, so that won't work. But I'm open Saturday night."

And that's an entirely *different* story!

~ ~ ~

Do you remember when you first met the person who would become your husband or wife? Those were exciting times, weren't they? Many of us look back with a certain fondness on those carefree dating days.

Except at the time, they weren't carefree at all! We worried about everything from where the date would be and how to dress, to how to impress the other person. We needed to be intelligent, spiritual, witty, interesting, communicative, accommodating, and an all-around well-balanced and likable person. No problem!

Did we say dating had been carefree? Better take that back. It was a pretty insecure time. As you began dating one person exclusively, you wondered if this person was "the one" for you. You wondered how and when you would know. Then, for Christian couples, there is the desire to remain pure even though temptation (and hormones) run high. There's so much to talk about and figure out.

If we're honest, many of us would not want to go back and do *that* all over again. Yet many things about our dating experiences were good. And we want to help you recapture the good aspects of the dating experience—the romance, the surprise, the fun, the undivided attention, the discovery—in your marriage.

But here's how it will be different from your earlier dating experiences. The person you're going to date:

- doesn't care how much you spend or how well you dress. He or she is used to you and loves you. Just being alone with you is treat enough!
- has already seen you at your very worst—and loves you anyway.
- doesn't need to be impressed—because he or she loves you already.
- already knows that you're intelligent, spiritual, witty, interesting, communicative, accommodating, well-balanced, and likable—just maybe not all at the same time!

Wow! Who wouldn't want to date *this* person?

You see, that person is your spouse—your mate for life. That person spoke marriage vows with you some years ago and wants to keep them. That person has lived with you through ups and downs, through job success and job loss, through joy and sorrow, and for many of you, through kids and diapers. That person knows you inside out. That person loves you.

And that person would like to have some special time alone—with *you!* That person would like to go on a date.

## Make a Date for a Date

Dating your husband or wife will be very different from dating a *potential* husband or wife. Yet it is just as important. When you were single, dating was a time to get away alone, to talk, laugh, and have fun together. You took time to learn more about each other, about your past and your dreams for the future. You gradually felt at ease with each other.

But, you see, even though you're married, the two of you still need the same thing. You need to get away alone and *continue to* talk, laugh, and have fun together. You need to learn *more* about each other, your past and your dreams for the future. You need to feel at ease with each other *as you face new challenges together*.

That's why dating shouldn't stop with marriage. Too often, married couples get settled, caught up in the routine of jobs, church, parenting, and other commitments. Many couples are so busy that they don't take time to nurture the foundation of their family—their marriage and their relationship with each other. As we know all too well, when that marriage foundation begins to crumble, everything else comes down with it.

Your marriage is your most important relationship after your relationship with God. Your marriage needs nurturing. Like a plant needs water or a car needs an oil change, your marriage needs consistent attention. It needs care and nurture every day; it needs a special "tune-up" once in a while. And that's why we wrote this book. Designed to be a companion to our book *The Five Love Needs of Men and Women,* this book will help to jump-start a habit that needs to be a regular part of your marriage. You need to reconnect with your spouse. You need to work at your marriage.

Guys, you wouldn't think of ignoring your car for a year at a time, so why do you think your wife can go for days or weeks at a time without attention from you? Women, you wouldn't think of buying a plant and refusing to water it, so why do you think your husband can go for days or weeks at a time without some of his most important needs being met?

Keeping a marriage together and the romance alive takes time. It means making one's marriage and spouse a priority and setting aside time for only him or her. In other words, it means planning dates on a regular basis.

This book will give you the motivation and ideas to plan a date for a date with your favorite person—your mate!

*~ Chapter Two ~*

# Dating with a Purpose

Our book *The Five Love Needs of Men and Women* describes the top five love needs of men and women from a survey we took of more than seven hundred couples. Our survey consisted of twenty love needs that we've been able to discern during Gary's years in marriage counseling and what we've heard from our national radio program listeners and thousands of couples at conferences. We asked each person to rank, in order of importance, what each felt he or she needed from his or her spouse. Following are the top five responses from those seven hundred couples (1,400 people).[1]

| Husbands' Top Five Love Needs | Wives' Top Five Love Needs |
| --- | --- |
| 1. Unconditional Love and Acceptance | 1. Unconditional Love and Acceptance |
| 2. Sexual Intimacy | 2. Emotional Intimacy and Communication |
| 3. Companionship | 3. Spiritual Intimacy |
| 4. Encouragement and Affirmation | 4. Encouragement and Affirmation |
| 5. Spiritual Intimacy | 5. Companionship |

[1] The chart is taken from Gary and Barbara Rosberg, *The Five Love Needs of Men and Women* (Wheaton, Ill.: Tyndale House, 2000), 8.

We found it interesting that as different as we know men and women are, the top five love needs for both husbands and wives are remarkably similar, but they often are given slightly different priority and are expressed—and met—in different ways.

The chapters in this book correspond with the top five love needs for the husband and the top five love needs for the wife. If you are a husband, you'll use part 2, where you will find Barb's advice for how you can meet your wife's top five love needs through four suggested dates for each need. We figured that because Barb understands some of the unique needs of women, she can help you plan a date that will touch your wife in a special way. If you are a wife, you'll use part 3, where you will find Gary's advice for how you can meet your husband's top five love needs through four suggested dates for each need. Again we figured that because Gary can talk about some of the unique needs of men, he can help you find effective ways to meet those needs.

We are working from the results of our survey. However, the needs you and your spouse have may be slightly different from our survey results. You may want to look over the results of the original survey that we gave these couples and then decide how you and your spouse would rank the needs (see appendix).

After you both rank your needs, make your own "top five" lists for each of you. This book will still be helpful because the dates we have suggested are meant to be starting points. We hope that as you read this book and study the suggested dates, you'll be inspired to go on dates that meet the specific love needs of your spouse. You can then be creative, tweaking any of these dates to make them work for you.

## Making It Count

If you and your spouse are not currently dating, we want to help you get into that habit. The two of you really do need time to reconnect and continue to stoke the fires of the romance that brought you together in the first place. Your marriage needs to be strong to withstand the onslaughts of daily life. When you know that you both are on the same team working toward the same goals and cheering each other on, then even the toughest competition won't be too much to handle.

If you already are in the habit of going on dates, we say, "Good for you!" Now we're going to spice up your lives a bit. Perhaps only one of you initiates the dates and handles the details. This book spreads that around: the wife plans dates for her husband, and the husband plans dates for his wife. And we have specifically designed these dates to meet each of the love needs for each spouse.

You might be asking, "Okay, Gary and Barb, why the focus on love needs? Why can't we just go to dinner and a movie?" Well, you can, and that's a good place to start. But if you're going to go out to dinner and a movie and spend the money on the date and a baby-sitter anyway, then make the date count! It's what we call having a "date with a purpose." Intentionally give your time together a purpose beyond just sharing an event. Focus on your mate's love needs. Put him or her in the spotlight and nurture your marriage relationship.

Why is it so important to meet your spouse's love needs? Well, let's start with something very basic. Way back when—months, years, or decades ago—you made a promise, a vow. If you said the traditional vows, you promised to love, honor, and cherish. If you wrote your own vows, you probably said something very similar. In any case, your vows communicated care and concern for the other person. In order to keep that vow, you need to unselfishly seek to meet your spouse's needs. You already take care of each other in many ways. Love needs are no different; they're just not as obvious.

When you meet your spouse's love needs, you're doing what God calls you to do by loving sacrificially. You are building a great marriage (who doesn't want that?). And, on the down-side, if you don't meet your spouse's love needs, then you leave plenty of opportunities for Satan to get in there and ruin your marriage by seeing that *someone* or *something else* steps in to meet those needs. When you meet your spouse's love needs, you're guarding your marriage against temptation, you're putting a hedge of protection around it.

### If You're Going It Alone

Dating your mate sounds like a terrific idea, right? Most of us would agree. But some of you may be saying,

- "That's okay for other couples, but I just don't think my spouse is going to respond."
- "He just seems to be stuck in a rut."
- "She doesn't like change. Routine is her way of thinking about everything, including dates."
- "We have some unresolved pain that needs to be addressed before we could go out and have a date."
- "We really can't afford much."
- "The kids are so demanding, how can we possibly put energy into dating?"

Or you may feel like Sherry, who called in to our radio program with this question: "I really care about my marriage, but my husband doesn't seem to be interested in our relationship. Do these dating ideas apply to me since I'm the only one who seems to be willing to work on our marriage?"

We would say to people like Sherry, "Don't lose hope." It sometimes takes only *one* person to begin to get the ball rolling in changing the quality of a marriage. Remember, God has made you one with your husband or wife. And in that oneness, each spouse is sensitive to the slightest actions—both the good and the bad—of the other.

Think about how much your husband or wife can benefit as you work at investing in your relationship. When you are willing to choose to do the right thing—when you are willing to be obedient to God and follow his principles of consistently and creatively loving, honoring, and cherishing your mate, regardless of his or her response—two things will happen. First, your character will be shaped more into the likeness of Christ. And second, your faithfulness to God will have an amazing impact on your mate.

So if your husband or wife resists you at first, stay diligent. You will eventually influence your relationship. Why? Because you're doing the godly thing!

Each time we encounter a difficult situation in marriage, we have a choice: We can do the right thing, even if it costs a lot, or we can take the easy road. But when we opt out, we also miss the potential blessing.

We encourage you to try these date ideas as a way of loving your spouse more concretely. Affirm him or her as you begin, and start small, allowing the impact of the dates to stoke the home fires. Stay at it. Stay positive. We know it will be worth it!

## How to Get the Most out of This Book

As noted above, this book is divided into parts including one part for the husband and one part for the wife. (Yes, you can peek at the other part if you want, but you might ruin a big surprise! You would probably be better off staying in your own part and working on the dates *you* want to plan!)

Husbands, you'll find help in part 2. There Barb summarizes the material in *The Five Love Needs of Men and Women* for each of the top five love needs of wives. Then she suggests four *Date Ideas* that you can plan for your wife in order to meet each love need.

Wives, you'll find help in part 3. There Gary summarizes the material in *The Five Love Needs of Men and Women* for each of the top five love needs of husbands. Then he suggests four

*Date Ideas* that you can plan for your husband in order to meet each love need.

For example, the wife's number four love need is "Encouragement and Affirmation." For that particular love need, we have offered the husband four different types of dates from which he can choose one that will help to meet his wife's need for encouragement. Why do we suggest four dates? Well, people are different. We realize that there are different lifestyles and different areas of the country (some people simply can't go into the city to a museum, for example, because the nearest museum is eight hours away!). People are at different stages—some have little children, some have difficult work schedules. People have different financial situations (we don't suggest flying to Paris for romance—although you can do that if you want!). The point is to jump-start your thinking.

In addition, each date in this book is rated for

- *flexibility* (Can I reschedule this easily if our plans get interrupted?)
- *ease of preparation* (How much is involved in putting this together?)
- *expense* (How much will this cost?)

In general, we try to provide a series of four dates with a few of them being very affordable, one medium, and one pricey (a pull-out-all-the-stops kind of date).

Each date includes a checklist called *Prep Steps* to help the husband or wife get the date planned. Sometimes those few steps can be the hurdle that prevents the date from happening, so we want to help. Unforgettable dates need preparation.

The husband can choose the date that seems most workable and then tweak what we suggest to work for him and his wife. He can do one date or all four (maybe his wife *really* needs encouragement!). But he ought to try to do at least one date for each love need over the course of a year. (If his wife also does her five dates for him, then they'll have dated ten times, or about once a month for a year. Not bad for starters.) We have put the chapters in order from the number five need to the number one need. But you can do the dates in any order.

But wait! There's more! Each section includes some *Pre-Date Ideas*. These will help you to begin thinking about what you want to accomplish on this date and why it is so important. The Pre-Date Ideas will help you get into the mind-set of thinking about this particular love need of your spouse and how to meet that need.

After each series of four Date Ideas we have included a few *Unforgettable Tips* that will help make the date, well, unforgettable. These are merely starters to help get you thinking. Use them, or do something even more unforgettable!

And finally, we also include some *Post-Date Ideas*. These are meant to help you continue to meet your spouse's love need after the date. You can't expect that this one date will meet the need for another year. Instead, you need to continue to be aware and to keep on being sensitive to meeting your spouse's love needs.

One more thing. At the end of each four-date section, we have included a series of discussion questions called *Let's Talk*. These questions are designed to be a part of your discussion during your date. They are divided into five levels—beginning with easy, nonthreatening questions (Level 1) and moving to in-depth, bare-your-soul questions (Level 5). These are focused on the particular love need and can be taken along on any one of the four dates for that need. You can pick and choose whatever questions are appropriate for you—again, these are merely discussion starters. The goal is to get you talking about the basic needs so that you come away from the date understanding your spouse a little more and being better able to meet his or her love needs.

To review, each chapter includes these features:

- Pre-Date Ideas
- Four Date Ideas, each with a Prep-Steps checklist
- Unforgettable Tips
- Post-Date Ideas
- Let's Talk questions

## So What Are You Waiting For?

That beautiful woman or dreamboat guy is already in your life—out there in the garage or at work or in the kitchen or with the kids. Your radar is tuned in to each other every day— but maybe the signal has been getting fuzzy. So ask your mate on a date.

Check out the ideas in this book. Find a time when you both can have a few hours together, and *put it on the calendar!* The rule is that nothing but an extreme family crisis can break any of these dates.

And we'll guarantee you something. When you ask your mate out on a date (and yes, it's okay for wives to ask out their husbands—in fact, we count on it here), we guarantee that you won't be turned down. We also guarantee something else. When you begin the habit of dating your mate, your marriage will become deeper, stronger, and happier.

# Part Two

# A Husband Plans Dates for His Wife

## ~Chapter Three~

# A Date to Meet My Wife's Need for Friendship

"Alan missed his plane?" Patti felt miserable. Together she and Bob had taken a day off work and driven two hundred miles in hopes of picking up their son at the Kansas City airport. They had anxiously waited, and now she was heartsick that he hadn't made the connection.

Bob and Patti stood alone at the empty gate, where moments earlier they had been bubbling with excitement, anticipating seeing their son walk off the plane. She tried to hold back tears and pressed her face onto her husband's shoulder. He gently patted her hair and soothed her by pulling her close into his arms.

Suddenly Patti heard the sound of Bob's quiet laughter, "Darling, let's make something good out of this trip after all. We've got a date! Come on. Let's go into the city. I'm disappointed, too, that Al didn't make his flight connection. But I'm glad that we get to be alone. We'll drive downtown and grab some dinner. I'm married to a fox, and this old guy isn't too old to show you a good time."

So Bob and Patti headed to a nice restaurant overlooking the plaza. At dinner they laughed together as Bob talked about the book he was reading. Patti, refreshed by the meal and Bob's idea to redeem the day, talked about several things that were important to her: a novel she was reading, their son, a problem she was having with a friend, and a project she was working on at her office.

Bob loved watching her face as she talked. She glowed with beauty.

Noticing his smile, she took his hand and said, "Bob, you don't know how important you are to me. I find you such a safe place to talk. When you listen to my heart, I gain so much confidence. I can say things to you that I can't say to anyone else. You are my best friend!"

## The Number Five Love Need of Women

Patti is right. Bob is her best friend. And he is aware that friendship is very important to his wife.

I thought it was very interesting that both husbands and wives rated friendship (companionship) in their top five love needs. For wives, the need rated number five; for men, the need rated number three.

While both men and women express a need for friendship/ companionship, they see friendship in marriage in very different ways. A husband will think of friendship as *doing* things with his wife. Admit it, guys. You probably think of friendship with your wife as taking her along on activities that you enjoy (and assuming that she enjoys those activities as well). Your wife, on the other hand, would probably say that she feels most like your friend when the two of you are sharing heart-to-heart communication, when you are having special time together to focus on just the two of you, or when you are dreaming of the future together. Washing the car together or cleaning out the garage together may not be her idea of friendship! Oh, she'll probably work with you, and she'll probably be glad the job is getting done—but it probably won't be meeting her love need for friendship.

Many of you have your male friends—guys who like to do the same things you do, such as watching sports, fishing, working on cars, or playing baseball. Those friendships are valuable to you, and you want to nurture them. You make time for your buddies; you enjoy their company.

Your wife is also your friend—in fact, she should be your best friend. You still need your male buddies to hang out with, and your wife knows that. But she also knows that she wants to be your very best friend. She wants you to want to spend time with her too. She wants you to value her, to care about your relationship enough to want to nurture it.

The kind of friendship your wife needs, however, is different from what your buddies need. She wants to feel complete security and trust in you. She wants to know that when she opens up to you with the confidential parts of herself, you will respond as a close and caring friend. You need to make your wife feel safe and accepted.

You need to be her best friend; she needs to be your best friend.

## Your Wife, Your Friend

Just as you have your buddies, your wife probably also has a set of women friends. These are the ones with whom she has lunch, does crafts, or goes to activities or exercise class. She may even consider a few of these women to be her *best* friends.

But she wants you as her *best* best friend. You see, her other friends may change or move away; you are there for the long haul. Her other friends see her at her best; you have been there at her worst. Because you are her *best* best friend, she knows that you will always be there for her, no matter what. You will be her companion through thick and thin—career changes, family changes, age, weight gain, graying hair, and wrinkles. You will be her companion for the rest of your lives. You will be doing things together for many years to come. You are an "unlimited" partnership, working together through the twists and turns of life.

Your wife needs to know that you enjoy being with her. She needs to know that she can feel safe with you. She needs to know that she can share absolutely anything with you—her ups and downs, her struggles and joys. She needs to hear that you have her very best in mind at all times. She needs to know that you will be there for her in the dark times, ready to wrap your strong arms around her and comfort her.

Integrity is an important part of friendship. Are you completely trustworthy? Does your wife know that she can trust you, that your word is your bond, that what you tell her is always the absolute truth? Are you the same person in public and in private? Your wife needs to know that she can trust you.

Your wife needs you to honor her. Too many women deal every day with husbands who belittle and berate them and everything they do. Friends don't do that to each other, so you should not do that to your wife. Speak lovingly to her, encourage her, brag about her in public, and respect her. I know from experience that a wife who is treated like this will blossom with poise and confidence. I guarantee it. And she will respond in kind to you.

## Showing Friendship and Companionship

Now that you know some of your wife's needs, let's consider some ideas about how you can meet them. (For a more complete treatment of this topic, read chapter 10 in our book *The Five Love Needs of Men and Women*.)

When you meet your wife's love need for friendship and companionship, you are creating a friendship that will literally last for a lifetime! Hey, since you're together anyway, why not have fun?

Of course, what is the basic fundamental of a good friendship? It is people who do things together. That's how friends are made—it's probably how you met your wife. So don't stop now—*do* things together. They don't have to be extravagant. Your wife just wants to be with you, and she wants to know that you want to be with her. Sometimes this "togetherness" can be a part of the daily routine. Instead of going separate directions on Saturday in order to get the errands run, do them together. At other times, togetherness can take the form of special dates or other activities that you plan and set aside the time to do.

Another part of friendship is security. Your wife wants you *with her* (that is, connected to her and looking out for her), and she wants you *committed to her* (that is, she needs to know that you will never leave her—emotionally, spiritually, or physically).

Friends also step into each other's worlds. They know about each other. They discuss what they're thinking, doing, reading, hoping. When was the last time you asked your wife about her goals, the book she is reading, her involvement at your kids' school, or how the committee she's on at church is going?

Friends talk about the past and the future. Often the best friendships are those that go way back, those that allow you to talk about the memories of times past. That is true for your friendship with your wife. Set aside times to talk about the past, remembering significant events you've shared. Consider how far you've come and how you've changed, both separately and together. Then look confidently to the future.

## Pre-Date Ideas

Before you consider the suggested dates in this section, I'd like you to think about your wife for a few minutes. Focus on the following questions:

_ Do I think of my wife as my best friend?
_ What kind of friend does my wife need me to be?
_ For my wife, the most important ingredient of friendship in our marriage is . . .

_ Does my wife feel safe with me?
_ Does my wife trust me? Am I always trustworthy?
_ Do I express an interest in my wife's activities? Do I really
  know what she does on this or that committee? Do I know
  what book she's currently reading? Do I communicate with
  my wife daily to hear her thoughts and feelings about her
  day and people she's involved with?

Do you want to be friends with your wife? Of course you
do. What drew you to her when you first met? What kind of
friendship did you develop in the early stages of your relationship? On what was it based? What can you do to rekindle that
friendship?

Look over the dates below, and see if you can find one that
you can make your own. Don't forget to bring along this book
or write down some of the discussion questions that appear at
the end of this date. These are to help you get a discussion
started about your wife's love need for friendship. What you
learn from her will give you information to take with you so
that you can continue to meet this love need for her every day.
Finally, look over the Unforgettable Tips and the Post-Date
Ideas that are included after the four Date Ideas.

Your wife may have lots of female friends, but she truly
wants you to be her best friend. As you consider the Date Ideas
below, think about what you can do to show her that you
consider her to be your very best friend—forever.

## Four Suggested Dates with Your Wife

**DATE IDEA #1**
# Out to Lunch
*(Rating: very flexible, easy to prepare, low to medium expense)*

Take your wife out to lunch. Whether or not she works
outside the home, every woman loves to have a "power lunch"

with her best friend. She will also love the fact that you are taking the time out of your day to be with her.

While it may sound easy, carefully consider your family and work situation and decide if you will need to plan ahead. It would be great if you could pop in on your wife and surprise her with an invitation to lunch, but you have to decide if that would be a good way to do it or if it would cause more stress for her.

This date obviously has its time limitations. You need to be sensitive to her time schedule at home or at work. If you are planning ahead, maybe you can plan for a longer lunchtime for you both. Take along the discussion questions, realizing that you may have to follow up on some later.

### Prep Steps

○ Get the date on both of your schedules. (If you want to try to surprise your wife, consider all the scenarios. If she is home with kids, you will have to cover baby-sitting. Take into account that she may need at least a little time to get ready to go out. If she works outside the home, consider how a surprise will affect her day. Does she already have a lunch meeting scheduled? She will *want* to be with you but may *have* to be somewhere else—not the scenario you want!)

○ Schedule a baby-sitter, if needed (a neighbor or friend often may be happy to do this for an hour or so at lunch-time).

○ Choose a place. If it's a popular place, make reservations so you don't end up standing in line.

○ Decide whether you're going to pick her up or have her meet you there.

○ Bring a red rose or a spray of her favorite flowers.

○ Select the Let's Talk questions you would like to discuss with your wife (write them down or mark them in this

book). Then take along either your list or this book so that you will remember what you want to talk about.

Choose an Unforgettable Tip and a Post-Date Idea from the lists at the end of the chapter.

**DATE IDEA #2**
# Dating Days
*(Rating: fairly flexible, may take some planning, probably inexpensive [unless you were a high roller when you were dating!] )*

Relive your early dating days, back when you were "just friends," remember? <u>What did you do together then?</u> Play tennis? Visit antique shops? Look through bookstores? Go for long walks? Visit art galleries? Play board games? Go hiking?

Now plan a date doing one of those activities—something that you enjoyed doing together as friends. If you used to enjoy spending time in bookstores on some of your early dates, then plan a date with your wife to do just that. She'll be thrilled to know that you're remembering those dating days so fondly and that you want to rekindle that friendship.

### Prep Steps
○ Get the date on both of your schedules—and the family master schedule.
○ Schedule a baby-sitter, if needed.
○ Depending on the type of date, consider what type of planning you need to do. Check on the opening and closing times for stores or galleries; reserve a tennis court, whatever.
○ Tell your wife what you'll be doing and why. She'll love it! And because of the wide variations that this date could encompass, she will want to know how to dress and what to expect. She'll spend the day anticipating this date with her own memories of those early dates with you.

○ Depending on the type of date, plan additional time to eat
out or go somewhere in order to be able to discuss the
questions. Make reservations, if needed.

○ Select the Let's Talk questions you would like to discuss
with your wife (write them down or mark them in this
book). Then take along either your list or this book so
that you will remember what you want to talk about.

Choose an Unforgettable Tip and a Post-Date Idea from the
lists at the end of the chapter.

**DATE IDEA #3**
# Hobby Lobby
*(Rating: flexible, may not take much planning, varies in
expense depending on the activity)*

Does your wife have a hobby that she is passionate about?
What does she do in her spare time? Is she constantly working
on scrapbooks? Is she an avid reader? Does she enjoy working
in the garden?

Depending on what her hobby is, get involved in it with
her. Work for an afternoon on her scrapbooks, and learn what
it is that she loves about it. Ask her to recommend a book she
has read recently; then read the book and discuss it with her.
Go out in the garden, and help her plant or weed. Find out
what she enjoys about her flowers and plants. After sharing in
her activities, spend some time talking about the Let's Talk
questions.

Maybe your wife doesn't really have a hobby. Talk to her
about something she'd like to learn to do. Has she expressed
an interest in learning photography? Have you both wanted to
take ballroom-dancing lessons? Here's a chance to do something together. Take a class, and learn how to do these things.
This may be more of a long-term commitment, but then so is
your marriage! Set aside some time early on to talk through
the Let's Talk questions.

## Prep Steps

○ Talk to your wife about her favorite things to do. If she has an obvious hobby, tell her you want to join her in that hobby for a day. Then be ready to learn! No fair turning on the big game or getting bored too quickly. Focus on your wife, and learn all that you can about her hobby and about her as you watch her at work. Do what you can to help.

○ If she doesn't have an obvious hobby, talk about what she might like to learn to do. Together keep an eye out for a class or whatever might fill the need. (Don't check this off until you have found it and signed up!)

○ Get the date for working on your wife's hobby or the date for the class(es) you'll be attending on everyone's calendar.

○ Schedule a baby-sitter, if needed.

○ Be sure to have ready whatever equipment you might need for the first class.

○ Select the Let's Talk questions you would like to discuss with your wife (write them down or mark them in this book). Then take along either your list or this book so that you will remember what you want to talk about.

Choose an Unforgettable Tip and a Post-Date Idea from the lists at the end of the chapter.

DATE IDEA #4

# "Benchmark" Weekend

*(Rating: not flexible, will take planning ahead, may be expensive)*

In our book *The Five Love Needs of Men and Women* I discussed the importance of creating "benchmark" times. By this I mean times when your focus is shared memories and the miles you've traveled in your marriage. It's a time to discuss life—

with all its sunshine and storms. Ideally, these benchmark times should come around every year or every couple of years. This provides a time to reconnect, to reflect, to celebrate, to reevaluate, and to adjust your friendship.

So for this date, create a benchmark time for your wife. Schedule an overnight or a weekend away. Go far enough that it almost feels like a vacation. Make your destination a surprise if you can.

I'd suggest a cozy bed-and-breakfast. You can find tons of such places by doing a little research on the Internet or in B & B directories at the library. Make reservations. Plan to leave early enough on a Friday to have time that evening for a nice dinner and talk. Then see what else comes along to enjoy the next morning in the locale. Shop the little shops with your wife. Check out the antiques. Try some new kind of food. Do these things together, and build a memory—a friendship memory.

### Prep Steps

- ○ Find a weekend—at least a Friday night through Saturday—that you can get away. Get the date on both of your schedules and the family master schedule. The rule is that nothing can break this date except an extreme family crisis.
- ○ If you have children, you may need to schedule an overnight baby-sitter. Perhaps the kids can stay with grandparents. If your children are old enough, see if they can stay overnight with friends.
- ○ Tell your wife to pack her overnight bag. While you can be mysterious about the location, be sure she knows what kinds of clothing she will need. If you're planning a walk in the woods, be sure she knows to wear appropriate clothing. If you're also hoping for dinner in a nice restaurant, she needs to know to bring an outfit for that occasion as well. (Believe me—if you don't tell her, trying

to take her into a nice restaurant while she is still wearing
hiking boots will definitely ruin the mood you're trying
to create!)

○ Help the kids get all their overnight things packed, and
get them to their locations. Leave your cell phone
number or the number of the place where you will be
staying with whoever is watching your kids. Have those
people's phone numbers on hand as well.

○ Plan for this type of activity to be an annual event.

○ Select the Let's Talk questions you would like to discuss
with your wife (write them down or mark them in this
book). Then take along either your list or this book so
that you will remember what you want to talk about.

Choose an Unforgettable Tip and a Post-Date Idea from the
lists below.

~~~

### Unforgettable Tips

1. Purchase one of those necklaces or key chains designed
for "best friends." Half goes to one friend, half goes to the
other friend. During the date, give one half to your wife
as a gift; you carry the other half.

2. During the date, be sure to tell your wife that she is your
best friend and that you want to be her best friend forever.

3. Take a photo of your wife sometime during the date.
Later have the photo enlarged, and put it in a nice frame
to take to work with you. Have her take a photo of you
for the same purpose. If you can get someone to take one
of you together, do that too.

### Post-Date Ideas

1. Leave some notes for your wife in places you know she'll
find them during the day. Say, "You're my best friend" or
"Best Friends Forever."

2. On a night when you might usually be out with the guys, change plans. Tell the guys that you're going to hang out with your best friend tonight—and let your wife hear you say it.

3. Turn off the TV and say, "What shall we do together tonight?"

4. When you get home from work each night, give your wife a hug and kiss and tell her that you're glad to be home with her.

→ 5. If you have some photos of your dating days, pull them out, and enjoy an evening looking them over. Pull out your wedding pictures while you're at it.

6. Begin to act on at least one comment she made in your discussion.

## Let's Talk

Choose some questions/comments from each level to help guide your discussion during your date. This way you can learn more about how you can meet your wife's need for friendship/companionship.

**LEVEL 1:**

### Dip Your Toes into the Water

- "What are a few things I do that refresh you the most?"
- "What's your favorite hobby? When you have some free time, what do you like to do most?"
- "Tell me about the best vacation you ever had."
- "If you won an all-expense-paid trip to anywhere in the world, where would you go?"
- "What can we do to exercise together on a regular basis?"
- "What's your favorite sport? Why do you like it? Do you feel that you're good at it?"

**LEVEL 2:**
## Up to Your Ankles
- "Do you feel that I spend enough of my free time with you? What things do you feel cut into our time together?"
- "Before we were married, were your closest friends girls or guys? Why? Describe for me your best friend at that time."
- "Describe two of your favorite memories of things we've done together."
- "Have we learned any hard lessons in the last six months? If so, what are they?"
- "What do you enjoy most about your life? What would you like to change?"

**LEVEL 3:**
## Treading in Deeper Waters
- "If we were to read a book together, what kind would it be? Do you have any suggestions? How could we make the time?"
- "When you were an adolescent, how important to you was being popular? To what extent did you notice friends who were trying to be popular?"
- "What are some special activities you would like for the two of us to do together?"
- "Describe some dream accomplishments for yourself at ages forty, sixty, and eighty."
- "Who are currently your closest friends? Why?"
- "What item in our schedule would you most like to change?"

**LEVEL 4:**
## Bouncing on the Waves
- "Describe three ways we can enjoy each other more."
- "Let me read you this quote from Nels F. S. Ferre: 'The first general rule for friendship is to be a friend, to be open, natural, interested; the second rule is to take time for friendship.' In what ways am I or am I not open, natural,

interested in you? In what ways do I take time to just be your friend? How can I do this better?"
- "What would you think if we started to have weekly meetings to talk through our schedule, the kids, the bills, the future, etc.? What day and time would be best for this?"
- "In what ways do you look forward to growing old together?"
- "What is it about female friendships that sometimes make them deeper than marriage friendships?"
- "What three things can we start doing to become better friends?"

**LEVEL 5:**
## Diving in Head First
- "What kinds of 'unexpected' things might I do to spice up our relationship?"
- "What do you think prevents couples from becoming (or staying) best friends? What three things could we do to become better friends?"
- "Let's talk about some of the ways we've tried to stimulate growth in our relationship before quitting because we got lazy or too busy. Which one of these could we start again with a renewed vision for what it was meant to accomplish?"
- Tell your wife in what ways you see her reaching her fullest potential. Tell her what gifts you see in her life, and offer some encouragement for her to use those gifts.
- "Do you think of me as your *best* best friend? If not, what can I do to be a better friend to you?"
- "Do you feel safe with me? Do you trust me? If not, why not? What can I do to help you feel more safe? What can I do to help you trust me?"

# ~ Chapter Four ~

# A Date to Meet My Wife's Need for Encouragement and Affirmation

It was one of those days, a tough one for a teacher. The students were uncharacteristically wild, and worse yet, it was the day Melissa's principal, Dan, evaluated her job performance.

Her husband, Rich, heard the discouragement in her voice as she told him during dinner what had happened. She described the out-of-control afternoon in the classroom. She recounted what the principal had said about her work. She wondered aloud whether she had chosen the right career and expressed doubts about her ability to handle the task of teaching. "I put so much of myself into those kids. I don't think Dan understands the amount of work and preparation I put into the classroom."

Rich listened patiently, not interrupting his wife as her thoughts and feelings spilled out. He looked in her eyes as she talked, trying to warm her with his smile. He knew he could argue with her about her negative perspectives about herself; he knew how capable she was. But he also knew that was not what his wife needed.

Rich leaned over and took her hand. "Melissa, you are an incredible woman. I appreciate you so much. Not only are you the most qualified and competent first-grade teacher that any twenty-three kids in the state could have, but you are also an incredible wife and mother. In addition to pouring yourself into those kids, you pour yourself into me and our kids. You make this house a welcome place to come home to. You find the energy to make my favorite foods. I'm inspired when I watch you around the kids at school. How did I ever get a woman like you to love a guy like me?" Her eyes softened as she took in her husband's words.

He stood and motioned for her to come into his arms. As he held her, he continued, "Besides, in my book you reign as queen. I can't imagine any woman being a better wife. I love you, and frankly, isn't that all that counts?"

The next morning at breakfast Melissa found a shoe box with "Mel" scribbled on it. Inside it were six paper towels on which Rich had made a list of 220 things he loved and admired about her!

As she read the list, she alternately smiled and cried. "Oh, Rich, your love is all that matters. This means the world to me."

"I would have gone on, but six towels were all that were left on the roll!" Rich said and laughed.

Melissa couldn't find a tissue to wipe her tears, so Rich took one of the paper towels and gently dabbed her face with it.

Rich knows how to encourage his wife.

## The Number Four Love Need of Women

Men and women have basically the same top five love needs—as you can see from the chart on page 11. The key difference is in their order. However, both husbands and wives ranked the need for encouragement and affirmation as number four. Yet, men and women are encouraged in different ways. The way *you* need others to encourage you may not be how *your wife* needs others to encourage her. You need to be sensitive to your wife's special need for encouragement in ways that will speak to her.

What is encouragement? The word literally means "to give courage; to inspire with courage, spirit, or hope; to hearten." This is what your wife needs from you.

You may be asking where your wife needs courage. Well, it helps if you know her well. Does she have a job that requires her to step out of her comfort zone? Is she leading a Bible study at church but feeling a little uncomfortable? Is she home with young children, needing the courage to know that she is making a good choice? Your wife needs your en*courage*ment. She wants you, her best friend, to give her the courage she needs to meet the challenges she is facing. She needs your words of inspiration. She needs you to give her hope for the future.

You won't believe it, guys, but trust me on this. You have incredible power—perhaps more than we wives might like to admit. When we feel completely worn out, exhausted, or burdened, a touch from you and a word of sincere encouragement can give us a boost of energy and a surge of hope that helps us to get back out there again.

Yet, there is also great power in negative words. You can probably remember someone's cutting, critical words to you from many years ago. Those words still hurt. If your wife is hearing only criticism from you, she is being *dis*couraged, not *en*couraged. Those negative comments weigh heavily on her. If you are in the habit of spewing negativity toward your wife, you will need to ask God to help you to grow that fruit of the Spirit called self-control. You will need to learn to measure your words.

I can tell you something: your positive words will have far more effect than your negative ones. Do you want to help your wife become a better person, become all that she can be, all that you *know* she can be? Then give her positive words. Feed her with encouragement. You will see a change immediately.

## The Courage to Encourage

Sometimes we get so wrapped up in ourselves, don't we? We wives know that your days are often tough (and we're going to be taking you on dates to help meet *your* need for encouragement). But we need you to recognize that what we do is important, too, and that we often feel stressed-out by our commitments, overwhelmed by our responsibilities, and exhausted by our schedules. We need you to have the courage to look at us for a moment.

Look at what we do for you. Consider the responsibilities we have as stay-at-home moms spending the day chasing toddlers and watching *Sesame Street.* Think about how much we do to keep the household running smoothly: doing laundry (those clean clothes don't just reproduce in the drawers!); planning, shopping for, preparing, and cleaning up after meals. Or consider the time it takes us to work outside the home and come home to more work. Think about the committees we serve on, the responsibilities we shoulder at school and church. Watch us as we deal with the children after school and dust off algebra skills in order to help a child with homework. Watch us juggle the family schedule and get people where they need to be on time. See how we handle preparations for guests. And if you want to see a marathon, stand back as we prepare for Thanksgiving and Christmas.

Granted, maybe you are a big help in some of these areas. But admit it, sometimes you are not. Your wife does it, and she does it flawlessly, seemingly with ease. You don't have to think about it because it gets done.

So, what do you need to do? Say *thank you!*

Tell your wife that you appreciate the fact that she handles this, that, and the other so easily. Thank her for all that she does to make your life easier. Thank her for taking some of that burden from you so that you can focus on other things.

She needs you to notice and appreciate her efforts. Even if

everything runs smoothly, that doesn't mean you aren't needed. It also doesn't mean that because she can handle it, you can work seventy hours a week. Instead, your wife needs you to appreciate all of this so much that you want to spend time alone with her on a regular basis just to let her know it.

## Giving Encouragement and Affirmation

In order to meet your wife's need for encouragement and affirmation, you will need to take the time to understand her. Study your wife. Find out where she most needs your encouragement. Consider how you can affirm her. Reflect her love language back to her. In other words, think about how she communicates her love and appreciation of you. Does she say she loves you? Is she always bringing little gifts to you? Does she express her love through touch? Whatever she is doing to affirm you is the way she will "hear" it when you affirm her. So mirror her actions back to her.

Let her talk through her situations; allow her to vent her frustrations at work or in her other responsibilities. Listen. Don't try to solve the problem; just let her talk and, yes, even cry. I call that letting her "drain the pain." Tears are a good release for your wife and can help her cleanse her system. After a good cry, she can often see her situation more clearly and be ready to hear your advice.

Give your wife first place in your life. Let her know that she is the most important person in your world. Sure, go out with the guys once in a while, but make sure your wife gets even more time in your schedule than they do! Watch the big game, but make sure your wife knows that when the TV goes off, your focus will be on her. When she knows she is not being overlooked or taken for granted, when she knows that you are going to be spending special time with her (and you look forward to it), then she will be truly encouraged.

Affirm her gifts. Let her know the potential that you see in her. Encourage her to develop those gifts. Provide the opportunity. Maybe she wants to take a class in a new skill. Take care of the kids when the class meets.

Appreciate her contribution, understand all that she does for you, and thank her for every single part of it.

In our book *The Five Love Needs of Men and Women* we discuss three different kinds of women. Your wife may be an independent woman, an insecure woman, or a balanced woman—and your offers of encouragement may need to vary slightly depending on the kind of woman your wife is. For further discussion of this topic, please see chapter 8 in our book.

## Pre-Date Ideas

Before you consider the suggested dates in each section, ask yourself a few questions:

_ Do I really know all that my wife does for me (and the family)?

_ Do I thank her?

_ Are my words to her full of praise and encouragement, or are they more often critical and impatient?

_ Can I sense when my wife is feeling stressed? How do I help her to cope?

_ Does my wife ever feel taken for granted?

_ Does she think that she is number one to me?

_ Do I know her gifts? Am I encouraging her in those gifts?

Your desire for this date is to show your wife that you *don't* take her for granted. This will be your way to thank her, to let her know that she holds first place in your life and in your heart. Except, you know what? Don't wait until this date night to do it. As part of your preparation, begin to thank your wife for something every day. As you begin to offer her encouragement and praise, it will get easier and become more natural.

You know all of your wife's strengths and weaknesses. You know her completely. You can be her Barnabas, her encourager—willingly forgiving her faults, encouraging her good points, and being with her all the way.

Look over the Date Ideas below, and see if you can find one that you can make your own. Bring along this book, or write down some of the discussion questions that appear at the end of this date. These are to help you get a discussion started about your wife's love need for encouragement and affirmation. What you learn from her will give you information so that you can continue to meet this love need for her every day. Finally, look over the Unforgettable Tips and the Post-Date Ideas that are included after the four Date Ideas.

*Four Suggested Dates with Your Wife*

**DATE IDEA #1**

## Picnic with a Twist
*(Rating: flexible, easy to plan, low expense)*

Plan a picnic with a twist—a picnic you can do any time of the year. Get your wife out of the house for a while—either come home early while she is still at work, or come up with some other way to have her gone for a while (make sure she's doing something fun, not grocery shopping!).

When she returns, have a picnic set up on a blanket in the living room. Have candlelight, a picnic basket, and a simple meal that you'll both enjoy. Believe me, guys, if you do this, she'll love it even if you're serving crackers and peanut butter! As you enjoy your picnic, spend some time talking through your Let's Talk questions.

### Prep Steps
○ Decide on a day to do this so you can plan to be home early, and be there when your wife arrives home. Or plan

for a Saturday, when you can send her out for the day.
Tell her not to come home until a certain time because
you'll have a surprise waiting. Perhaps arrange with one
of her friends to take her out for a while (that way she
won't change her mind about going out). Put this on
your calendar.

○ If you have children, plan for them to be away so you
won't be interrupted. Have them stay at their friends'
houses for a couple of hours. Contact those friends'
parents, and work this out ahead of time.

○ Find a blanket. Dig out the picnic basket if you have one.

○ Decide on the meal. You can prepare something simple,
or purchase it from a local deli.

○ While your wife is gone, move furniture from the living
room, if necessary. Set up your picnic area, light some
candles, play some music (perhaps one of those "nature
sound" CDs or tapes with sounds from the forest; you can
find these at your local library), and set out your basket.

○ Select the Let's Talk questions you would like to discuss
with your wife (write them down or mark them in this
book). Then take along either your list or this book so
that you will remember what you want to talk about.

Choose an Unforgettable Tip and a Post-Date Idea from the
lists at the end of the chapter.

**DATE IDEA #2**
## Dinner Fit for a Queen
*(Rating: flexible, fairly easy to plan and prepare, low to medium
expense)*

Do you like to cook? Are you a whiz in the kitchen? If not, are
you a connoisseur of good food? Maybe you would love to go
out to a really nice restaurant, but there's never the time or the
money. Well, here's a chance to have a terrific meal without a
lot of expense.

As with the date above, this will all happen in the comfort of your own home, where you will provide an elegant meal for your wife. Send her out for a while, as with the date above, or surprise her at the end of a long workweek. When she gets home, cover her eyes, take her to your bedroom, and tell her to dress in her favorite best dress or evening gown. Then you'll put on your best clothes. When you're dressed, take her arm and lead her to the "restaurant" (your kitchen or dining room), where you have set the table with your best china, linens, and candles. Have soft music playing. Maybe do some dancing. Then enjoy a wonderful meal and conversation.

### Prep Steps

○ Decide on a day to do this so you can plan to be home early and be there when your wife arrives home. Or plan for a Saturday, when you can send her out for the day. Tell her not to come home until a certain time because you'll have a surprise waiting. Perhaps arrange with one of her friends to take her out for a while (that way she won't change her mind about going out). Put this on your calendar.

○ If you have children, arrange for them to be away for the evening. Have them stay at their friends' houses for a while or overnight. (Offer to reciprocate.) If your children are young enough, put them to bed early.

○ Prepare your menu, shop, and cook. Otherwise, call a local restaurant and order a couple of meals to go. Don't forget about dessert! (Chocolate is always a winner!)

○ Set the table with a tablecloth, your best china, linens, and candles. Put on some music.

○ If you already know what you want your wife to wear, lay it out on the bed. Then decide what you will wear.

○ Select the Let's Talk questions you would like to discuss with your wife (write them down or mark them in this

book). Then take along either your list or this book so that you will remember what you want to talk about.

Choose an Unforgettable Tip and a Post-Date Idea from the lists at the end of the chapter.

### DATE IDEA #3
# A Day of Pampering
*(Rating: not flexible, fairly easy to plan, expensive)*

Set aside a day to completely pamper your wife. Make reservations for her at a salon for a complete pampering (this is not just a hair salon, in case you're not up on this; it's a place where she can get a facial, a manicure, a pedicure, and maybe more). Or send her for a massage. You want to really score points? Include a trip to the mall for a new outfit.

Don't tell her about this ahead of time. Just have her set aside the day.

On the morning of the special day, bring her breakfast in bed. On the tray, include a certificate describing her schedule for the day. Then send her on her way. While she's gone, clean up the house and clean out the car. Your lady of leisure deserves to feel like a queen even when she comes home!

When she returns, take her out for a wonderful meal (in the clean car). She can wear her new outfit. You might even want to go someplace where you might run into people you know . . . so you can show her off a bit! Do your Let's Talk questions during your dinner.

### Prep Steps
○ Tell your wife you're planning a special day for her, and agree on a date.
○ Make the appointment for your wife. Prepay for her. If possible, go ahead of time, and give the salon owners a red rose to give to your wife from you when she arrives.
○ If you're including shopping in the certificate, tell her

that you want her to go shopping. Then set a time for her to return so that you can go out to eat.

○ If you have children, arrange for baby-sitting for the time you'll be out for dinner.

○ Make dinner reservations.

○ Clean the house and car. If appropriate, enlist the help of your children, explaining to them why you're doing what you're doing.

○ Select the Let's Talk questions you would like to discuss with your wife (write them down or mark them in this book). Then take along either your list or this book so that you will remember what you want to talk about.

Choose an Unforgettable Tip and a Post-Date Idea from the lists at the end of the chapter.

**DATE IDEA #4**

# Guys Honoring Their Wives
*(Rating: not flexible, will take planning, may be expensive)*

Is your wife a really social person? Maybe you two have quite a bit of time together, but you really don't get out with others much—and perhaps that's what your wife is starving for. So guys, here is your mission should you choose to accept it.

Contact the husband(s) of your best friends. Get the guys together to plan a date for your wives. Each of the husbands needs to be clued in on what you're planning—that this is an encouragement date for your wives. If they're interested, don't let anyone off the hook until a date is on the calendar for all of you. (Of course, all of them will say, "Let me check with my wife." Follow up until everyone has the date on the calendar, including the wives. All the wives need to know is that there will be a special get-together.)

Now guys, don't plan this get-together at any of your homes. That will not be a pleasant surprise for one wife in particular. Be creative. Come up with something that all of the wives will enjoy.

In addition to the activity, each husband should prepare a little speech of encouragement for his wife so that he can brag about her in front of everyone. Share with each other what you might say ahead of time so that all of you guys will be on the same page (no one wants to be "one-upped" in this situation!). Use your imagination.

You'll need to set aside some time after the date to work through your Let's Talk questions in private.

### Prep Steps

○ Contact the guys, and get the date on everyone's calendar. Remind the guys that they need to handle the baby-sitting arrangements, if needed.

○ Decide on an activity. Make reservations, if needed.

○ Be sure the guys are clear on how their wives need to dress—no wife wants to be embarrassed when she goes out with others. So agree ahead of time, and then pass along that information to your wives.

○ Prepare your speech for your wife. Remind the rest of the guys to prepare their speeches.

○ Select the Let's Talk questions you would like to discuss with your wife (write them down or mark them in this book). Then take along either your list or this book so that you will remember what you want to talk about.

Choose an Unforgettable Tip and a Post-Date Idea from the lists below.

~~~

### *Unforgettable Tips*

1. At some point on your date, take both of your wife's hands in yours, look into her eyes, and thank her for everything she does for you. Acknowledge her sacrifices, affirm her love for you and the family. Then praise her

for who she is, not necessarily just what she does. Quote to her from Proverbs 31:29, "There are many virtuous and capable women in the world, but you surpass them all!"

2. In the course of a day while she is out (this will work well on your picnic day or meal-at-home day), do at least one chore that she has been wanting you to do. (I'm sure you can figure out what to do if you think real hard!) Then attach a bow to the chore—tie a bow around what had been a leaky faucet or on the door of the now clean study—and put a note there that says, "Just because I appreciate all you do for me!"

3. Enlist your kids' help. Kids of almost any age can do this. Have them cut out lots of red hearts from construction paper. On each heart, write one thing that you and the kids most appreciate about your wife. Have the kids contribute and write on several paper hearts. Hang or lay the hearts around the house.

### Post-Date Ideas

1. Try out one of these phrases each day with your wife. You'll be glad you did.
   - "You're the best wife a husband could ever have."
   - "You're the most wonderful woman in the universe!"
   - "Have I told you lately that you're my hero?"
   - "I love growing old with you."

2. Leave little thank-you notes around the house, thanking her for what a good job she does in the many responsibilities of her life.

3. Brag about your wife to your friends. Sincerely compliment something about her in front of other people.

4. When you catch your wife's eye across a crowded room, smile and wink at her.

5. Begin to act on at least one comment she made during your discussion.

## Let's Talk

Choose some questions/comments from each level to help guide your discussion during your date. This way you can learn more about how you can meet your wife's need for encouragement and affirmation.

**LEVEL 1:**

### Dip Your Toes into the Water

- "When do you feel most glad that you married me?" Then tell your wife when you feel most glad that you married her.
- Tell your wife what impressed you the most about her when you first started dating.
- "What is the best compliment I could give you?"
- "Do I say please and thank you enough for the little and big things you do? If I don't, how can I improve?"
- "In what areas do you want to feel more confident about yourself? How can I help?"
- "How do you like to be pampered?"

**LEVEL 2:**

### Up to Your Ankles

- "What types of little gifts would go a long way toward showing you how much I love and appreciate you?"
- "Name five things I could do that would pleasantly surprise you."
- "Do you ever feel that my compliments are hollow? If so, when is this the case, and how can I show you my sincerity?"
- "Do you think that you spend most of your time doing what you are well suited to do? If not, what needs to change? What would you most enjoy doing on a daily basis?"
- "What do you think your spiritual gifts are? How can you work at developing them, and how can I help you in this?"

**LEVEL 3:**
## Treading in Deeper Waters

- "Do you ever feel that I am critical of you? If so, how can I avoid that?"
- "When was the last time you cried? Why?"
- Tell your wife how often you think of her during the day. Explain how those thoughts of her make you feel.
- "What one thing that I do for you makes you feel truly loved and cared for?"

**LEVEL 4:**
## Bouncing on the Waves

- "When you try something and fail, how should I respond? What would be the most helpful to you?"
- "What does it mean to you to have a good self-image? What do you think of yourself . . . really?"
- "What gives you the motivation to get up in the morning? Do I help or hinder your zest for living?"
- "In what areas of your life do you feel most insecure? When you are feeling that way, what can I do to encourage and strengthen you?"
- "What can I do to help you bring out your natural talents and abilities? Do I ever suppress them, and if so, how?"

**LEVEL 5:**
## Diving in Head First

- Tell your wife in what ways and in what areas you see her reaching her fullest potential. Describe what her life is giving back to you, to your children, and to God.
- "What little or big things can I do to help make you feel that you're an extremely valuable person—to our home, to me, to our friends, to the church?"
- "Think about last week. What did I say to you that was positive and encouraging? What did I say to you that was critical and discouraging?"
- List five positive things you see in your wife in each of the

following areas: achievements, service to God and others,
special talents and skills, character qualities, and
childrearing.

- "Is there anything about life in general or our current
  circumstances that discourages or disappoints you? What
  can I do to help turn that around?"

*~ Chapter Five ~*

# A Date to Meet My Wife's Need for Spiritual Intimacy

Carrie was homesick. As newlyweds she and her husband, Terry, had moved halfway across the country to land the perfect job in northern California. But the holidays were approaching, and expenses were tight—which meant not going home to see family and friends over the holidays.

Carrie knew that she needed lots of strength from God to help her overcome the anguish of feeling alone in a new setting, and she shared that need with her husband. Terry knew he, too, needed wisdom and God's provision to weather the stress of a new job, a new location, as well as a new relationship to Carrie. So he kept a daily appointment with God by reading the Bible and spending time in prayer. One of Terry's mentors had told him that the best thing he could do to help his wife spiritually was to keep his own spiritual life vibrant.

Each morning Terry asked God for provision not only for himself but also for his wife. Wanting to keep his wife's needs a priority, he wrote at the top of each page in his daily planner, "Pray for Carrie's needs, and look for ways to help her grow spiritually."

One night when they were having dinner, Terry asked Carrie how she was feeling about being away from family and friends. The tears that filled her eyes said it all. He reached over, took her hand in his, and prayed softly, asking God to touch her pain and to comfort her in her distress. He felt her relax as he prayed, and the smile on her face when he was done praying encouraged him.

Carrie was comforted by her husband's spiritual provision for her, and their growing spiritual life eased her insecurity. She became more confident in their new setting. Terry's example of spiritual leadership in their home set the tone for Carrie, and after a few months she began a neighborhood Bible study, which proved to be a significant source of spiritual growth and satisfying relationships for her.

Terry's commitment to partner spiritually with his wife forged in their marriage a supernatural strength that would take them through the most difficult of times.

## The Number Three Love Need of Women

The love need for spiritual intimacy appeared in the top five for both men and women. Men ranked it number five; women ranked it number three. Clearly, Christian couples see themselves as more than just the two of them. They picture their marriage like a cord with three strands—God, husband, wife—inextricably woven together. And because of that, they are very aware of the spiritual dimension of their lives and of their marriage. From a wife's perspective, spiritual intimacy involves her husband's own spiritual growth, shared spiritual growth between her and her husband, communication about spiritual matters, and her husband's spiritual leadership in the home.

For women, spiritual intimacy is built on a foundation of trust. Of course, trust pops up in many of these love needs, but in the case of spiritual intimacy, a woman needs to know that her husband is completely trustworthy. Your wife needs to know that she can trust you in the areas of your own personal relationship with God and in your support of her spiritual growth. She also wants to be able to trust in your godly leadership through decisions that affect the family and in your spiritual upbringing of the children.

Sound like a lot of responsibility? You bet! Can you handle it? Of course. But you're not alone in this. God invites you to depend on his Spirit and power.

You assumed this responsibility when you got married. According to the Bible, you are the spiritual "head" or leader of your home. Most men want to be leaders, but few succeed at it. Many prefer to dictate without leading by example. An authentic leader leads by mentoring his wife and kids. Your wife doesn't want to be told what to do; she needs to be shown by your example. Real leaders of the home reach out when they see a need, offering to help. Your wife needs you to have a vibrant spiritual life, and she wants to watch as you experience God's grace firsthand. Then you will be ready to pass it on to others.

This kind of leadership involves much more than just bringing home the bacon. It involves building your wife's confidence that your words, actions, and decisions arise from your relationship to God, which you nurture through consistent Bible study and prayer.

Spiritual leadership does not mean that you must meet all of your wife's spiritual needs. Only God can do that. But your example can lead her to God, who can truly meet her needs. You can take the initiative by reading Scripture together, praying together, and having open discussion about your spiritual growth.

Granted, your wife may go ahead without you if you choose not to take the time to grow spiritually. Eventually, you may find her miles ahead of you, waving at you from the distance. (And you can bet she's doing lots of praying for you from over there!) But, believe me, she really doesn't want to be over there all by herself. She wants you by her side, even a couple of steps ahead. And guys, when you let your wife carry the spiritual responsibility in the home, you're missing out on a depth in your relationship that you won't find anywhere else. You're missing out on hearing her heartfelt prayers for you. You're missing out on the godly perspective and advice she can give. And you're missing out on meeting one of her most deeply felt love needs.

## Two Lives, One Holy Spirit

Think about it. When you are helping your wife to grow spiritually, you are helping her to be a great wife, a terrific mother, and a valuable servant of her Lord. And if you were to ask her, she'd probably say that those are some of her top goals in life. So by encouraging her spiritual growth, you're helping her to fulfill many of her own deepest desires.

Your wife needs to be growing spiritually because she is a child of God. She needs to care for her personal relationship with her Father. Obviously, *you* are not God, and you are not responsible for her growth. God is the source of her strength, her salvation, and her security. But your encouragement by your example, fervent prayer life, and continued growth and development as a man can cause her to become increasingly more tender and open toward growing spiritually. Encourage her to quench her spiritual thirst by having her own time to pray and study the Bible, by becoming part of a group Bible study, or by attending a women's conference. Don't let her off the hook if she says that she teaches Sunday school or is a small-group leader. So many women are so busy feeding others that they aren't being fed themselves. She needs to be given food and water for her *own* soul on a regular basis.

What does that mean for you? Perhaps you'll provide a few minutes of quiet time each day so she can have devotions. Maybe you'll need to watch the kids so she can go to a Bible study or a conference. Consider it a high honor to be able to encourage her in this way.

Your wife also needs fellowship with other Christians, but especially you—her best friend. You need to have a church that you call home. Join a small group that meets for prayer, study, or service. Think about having a couple's study with some friends. As the Christian adult who is with your wife most regularly, take the time to talk about spiritual things together. She longs for this kind of connection with you.

Is your wife expressing her spiritual gifts? One couple we know recently discovered that the wife has a strong gift of teaching. The women's Bible study at their church approached her to fill in for a teacher who had to be away on a trip. This wife threw herself into her assignment with relish and gave her lesson with the obvious hand of God. She loved it! The women loved it, too, so much that they added her to their team of teachers. She was a bit reticent at first—it would be a time commitment, one she might not be able to afford with her other responsibilities. In addition, some of her old insecurities took over—was she really worthy to stand up and teach anyone anything? But her husband told her that he had long seen this gift in her and was excited that someone else finally saw it and was able to do something about it. When she feels overwhelmed, her husband is there to encourage her, affirm her knowledge of God's Word, and tell her she's gifted by God and has a responsibility to use her gift for his glory.

Your wife will grow in her faith as she uses her spiritual gifts. If she doesn't know what they are, try to help her discover them. If she already knows, pray with her to discover how she might best use her gifts.

This may come as a surprise to you, guys, but one of the best ways to meet your wife's need for spiritual intimacy is for you to take on the mantle of leadership that God has given. (Now, it is important to understand that there are different types of leadership. In our book *The Five Love Needs of Men and Women,* I discuss the controlling leader, the passive leader, and the servant leader. Obviously, the first two are negatives, and your goal is to be a servant leader in your family. (Check out chapter 6 for more information.) You need to be your wife's spiritual sounding board. She needs to know that she can talk with you about spiritual things. Commend her spiritual strengths. Above all, lead a vibrant spiritual life yourself. Let her see that God comes first in your life (she'll gladly take second place to God!). Pray for her and with her. Let her see you read your Bible. Read it together.

Some of you may be saying, "Hey, we already do all that." Good for you! But I guarantee that many reading this book are saying, "Pray with my wife? Read the Bible with her?" Some of you know, deep down, that you want this too (remember, it's a love need of yours as well), but you just don't know where to begin. The next section will give you some thoughts, and our Date Ideas will give you even more opportunity to move naturally into this vital area of your lives.

## Pre-Date Ideas

Before you consider the suggested dates in each section, ask yourself a few questions:

- How would I describe my wife's personal relationship with Jesus Christ? What makes her tick spiritually?
- Does my wife have a daily time for Bible reading and prayer? When? How often does she pray?
- Does she consider me the spiritual leader of our household?
- How is my personal walk with God?
- What are my wife's spiritual gifts? How is she using them?
- Do I pray for my wife? How often? Do I know what my wife would like me to pray about for her?

Consider the rewards you will reap from meeting this love need for your wife. As the two of you grow closer together spiritually, that cord of three strands—the two of you and God—is woven ever more tightly. When you know that you can lean on each other for spiritual strength and godly guidance, you know that you can weather any stresses or storms that come into your marriage.

Even further, as your children watch this kind of love between the two of you, they will discover what they should look for in the future. They will see the absolute necessity of having a godly spouse. They will understand the power of prayer and of knowing God's Word. They will see that the Bible is indeed "full of living power" (Hebrews 4:12) and has words that apply to today and every day.

*Four Suggested Dates with Your Wife*

### DATE IDEA #1
# Get the Group Together
*(Rating: not flexible [it's on a regular night out], easy to prepare, low expense)*

If you are already attending a couples' Bible study of some kind, use the evening of that study for this particular date. Plan ahead with the other men at the Bible study. Tell them about this book and what you're doing. Ask if they would be up for a "celebrate our wives" night at Bible study. It should come as a surprise to the women. Tell the guys that they will have a couple of minutes to say something to their wives and to read a few verses to her.

Get together as usual, but suspend the lesson for that night. Have each man prepare ahead of time something to say about his wife. Have the wives share prayer requests. Have each husband and wife hold hands with each other. If your group is comfortable praying aloud, have each husband pray aloud for his wife. If not, have each couple pray quietly together.

Enjoy some dessert—that you *guys* brought! Set aside some

time later that evening or the next day to talk with your wife
about the Let's Talk questions.

### Prep Steps

○ Talk to the leader and the other guys in your Bible study
about planning this evening.

○ Ask the guys to prepare something to say to their wives—
give everyone an idea so all the guys are on the same
page. Have each one choose a few verses of Scripture to
read to his wife.

○ Tell the guys to keep it a secret.

○ Make sure one of the guys is prepared to provide a
dessert. If someone else had already been assigned to
provide the dessert, make sure you tell that person that
he or she doesn't have to do it for that week.

○ Select the Let's Talk questions you would like to discuss
with your wife (write them down or mark them in this
book). Then take along either your list or this book so
that you will remember what you want to talk about.

Choose an Unforgettable Tip and a Post-Date Idea from the
lists at the end of the chapter.

DATE IDEA #2
## A Day in God's Creation
*(Rating: needs to be flexible [you need good weather], easy to
plan, low expense)*

Get out into God's beautiful creation. Plan a day out with your
wife. Take along a picnic lunch—this can be as simple as sand-
wiches from the deli. Find a beautiful location where you will
be totally alone: on a hill above town, by the seashore, out in
the woods, or on a bridge overlooking a stream. Take along a
blanket and whatever else you need to have a comfortable
time. Sit and enjoy the beauty of God's handiwork and the
beauty of your wife. Take along the Let's Talk questions.

## Prep Steps

○ This can be fairly spontaneous because you will need to have nice weather. If on Friday the forecast is good for Saturday or Sunday, kick into gear with this. Tell your wife to plan for a couple of hours away.

○ Decide on your perfect location.

○ Schedule a baby-sitter, if needed.

○ Pack a blanket or some lawn chairs.

○ Decide what you'll want to take for lunch, and buy it ahead of time. Or on the way to the place you've picked out, stop at a deli and pick out things you both will enjoy.

○ Make sure your wife is dressed comfortably (take along sweatshirts if it might get chilly).

○ Select the Let's Talk questions you would like to discuss with your wife (write them down or mark them in this book). Then take along either your list or this book so that you will remember what you want to talk about.

Choose an Unforgettable Tip and a Post-Date Idea from the lists at the end of the chapter.

**DATE IDEA #3**

# A Special Birthday Surprise
*(Rating: not flexible, fairly easy to plan, medium expense)*

What better time to celebrate God's gift of your wife than on her birthday! If her birthday is coming up, great! Otherwise, wait to do this date, or just do it on her half-birthday, or three-quarters birthday, or 7/12 birthday (you know, the number of her birthday in whatever month you're in—at least then she won't be expecting it!). In any case, make it a birthday celebration—complete with a cake, decorations, and a gift. If you have children, you can involve them in this one. You can have them plan a meal and prepare it (if they're old enough), or you can take everyone out for dinner. In a special prayer, thank God for giving you the gift of your wife. Then give her a special gift from you.

If you're alone, talk about some of the Let's Talk questions. Otherwise, plan some time at home later to go over the questions.

### Prep Steps

○ Tell your wife to set aside some time to go out with you on a particular evening.

○ Make reservations at her favorite place to eat.

○ Decide if you're including your kids. If not, schedule a baby-sitter.

○ Purchase a gift for your wife—something very special that she will treasure.

○ Include a special dessert—birthday cake or her favorite dessert. If your children are old enough, they could stay home and decorate a cake while you and your wife are out. Then you could return home from dinner and have cake with the whole family.

○ Select the Let's Talk questions you would like to discuss with your wife (write them down or mark them in this book). Then take along either your list or this book so that you will remember what you want to talk about.

Choose an Unforgettable Tip and a Post-Date Idea from the lists at the end of the chapter.

**DATE IDEA #4**
# Commit a Kidnapping
*(Rating: not flexible, lots of planning, expensive)*

All right, guys. You're about to become guilty of a felony. That's right. You're going to kidnap your wife and take her away for the weekend.

Arrive home or at your wife's office, scoop your wife into

the car, and off you go. I promise, no police cars will be following.

The focus of this date is to be able to get away for an extended period of time. This will allow time for the important topic of spiritual intimacy—something that you have difficulty talking about, especially if you're trying to fit your discussion into a shorter time period. Some of the Let's Talk questions are pretty deep, and you may need the extra time to explore them sufficiently.

If you're finding that spiritual intimacy is a challenge in your marriage, this may be the best date for you. Spend time away so that you can read God's Word and pray together without the distractions of home, children, and telephones. This could be a way to jump-start a spiritual relationship that will last long after this weekend is over.

### Prep Steps

- ○ Decide on the target date. Check with your wife in rather noncommittal terms: "We have nothing going on such and such a date, do we? Well, keep it clear for now."
- ○ If she works outside the home, check with her boss about letting her off a couple of hours early. Check with your boss about the same.
- ○ Make reservations for dinner and your overnight stay.
- ○ Provide for baby-sitting for the children, if needed.
- ○ If you can pull it off, try to pack her luggage ahead of time so that the weekend away can be a complete surprise. Make a list of the clothing and makeup she'll need. If she's home all day and you can't pack her bag, then just call her an hour before you get home to clue her in slightly—just tell her to pack an overnight bag.
- ○ Pack some treats in the car for the ride to the location you've selected.
- ○ Select the Let's Talk questions you would like to discuss with your wife (write them down or mark them in this

book). Then take along either your list or this book so that you will remember what you want to talk about.

Choose an Unforgettable Tip and a Post-Date Idea from the lists below.

~~~

## *Unforgettable Tips*

1. If your wife needs, or would like, a new Bible, purchase one for her. (Or, with the large selection currently available, take her shopping so she can pick out one for herself.) You might want to get her a nice leather edition and have her name embossed on the cover. For the past few years I have used Tyndale's *One Year Bible,* which includes a daily reading from the Old Testament, New Testament, Psalms, and Proverbs. It helps me move through the entire Bible in a year.

2. If your wife already has a favorite, well-worn Bible, you might want to purchase a Bible cover for her.

3. Buy your wife a devotional book that will help her grow spiritually. Diane Eble's *Abundant Gifts* (Tyndale House) is a devotional daybook that celebrates and makes us aware of God's many gifts to us, including how we can use our gifts to help others.

4. At some point during your date, tell your wife that you are glad that God gave her to you.

5. Put "Pray for my wife's needs and spiritual growth" at the top of every page in your day planner. Then begin a discipline of praying daily for her. Show your wife your planner, and let her know that praying for her is your top priority every day.

6. Hold your wife's hands or wrap your arms around her and pray for her aloud.

7. Talk about a ministry that the two of you might be able to do together.

## Post-Date Ideas

- On Post-it notes or index cards, write out a Scripture verse that will remind your wife of God's love for her and his plan for her life. Every day or two during the next few weeks, leave a verse in a conspicuous place—the bathroom mirror, the refrigerator, in her purse, in her Bible. Let her know you're praying for her too.
- Call your wife at least twice a week, and ask her what you can pray about for her.
- Let your wife see you reading your Bible. Try to make time to read God's Word with her every day—even if it's only a few verses.
- Purchase a devotional book for couples, and begin to use it. Bill and Nancie Carmichael's *Lord, Bless This Marriage* (Tyndale House) is a yearlong devotional that includes Scripture, meditations, questions, and a prayer journal to record your spiritual prayer journey as a couple.
- Begin to act on at least one comment that she made during the date.

## Let's Talk

Choose some questions/comments from each level to help guide your discussion during your date. This way you can learn more about how you can meet your wife's need for spiritual intimacy.

### LEVEL 1:
*Dip Your Toes into the Water*
- "What are your favorite hymns or choruses? Why are they favorites?"
- "What one question will you be sure to ask God when you meet him?"
- "Do you think that we generally get involved with people who are good for us and for our relationship to one another

and to God? If you think some of our relationships are questionable, what should we do about them?"
- "What new Christmas or Easter tradition would you like to start this year?"
- "Tell me about your funniest camp or youth-group experience from your past."
- "What is your favorite part of our church service—the music, the sermon, the prayer times, the fellowship with other believers, or something else?"

**LEVEL 2:**
*Up to Your Ankles*
- You've probably heard about your wife's spiritual journey before, but ask her to tell you about it again.
- "What helps you grow closer to Christ? What things interfere with your spiritual life?"
- "Do you believe that God performs miracles today? In what ways? When was the last time a miracle happened to us?"
- "In what ways is our marriage a good example to our children (or to our friends)? What do you think our friends say about our marriage? Why? Are they right?"
- "If you could meet anyone in the Bible, who would it be? Why? What would you ask? What would you share?"

**LEVEL 3:**
*Treading in Deeper Waters*
- "What spiritual gifts do you think God has given you for serving him?" Then tell her what you see in her.
- "Are you satisfied with our level of involvement in our church and/or community? Why or why not? What needs to change?"
- "In what areas do we minister to others better as a team? In what areas are we better ministers as individuals? How can I be more supportive in the activities you do without me?"
- If she attends a women's Bible study, ask her about it.

"What are you studying? What is your role? Are you getting refreshed there? Why or why not?"

- "Do you have a daily time to pray alone and read the Bible? If so, when? If not, why not? What do you do during that time? How does it refresh you?"
- "What experiences have allowed you to believe in a kind and loving God? Is there anything in the world that causes you to doubt this?"

**LEVEL 4:**

### Bouncing on the Waves

- "In what ways do I treat you as a fellow heir in Christ? In what ways don't I?"
- "Are you satisfied about how I make decisions for our family? Why or why not? What can I do better?"
- "Are you satisfied with the time we spend together reading the Bible and praying? What can we do together to meet each other's needs in this area?"
- "Since conflict is inevitable in marriage, how are we doing in terms of resolving our conflicts? What can we do better?"
- "Do you have difficulty with the concept of me as 'head' of the household? Why or why not?"

**LEVEL 5:**

### Diving in Head First

- "In what ways am I encouraging you in your spiritual walk with God? What else would you like me to do?"
- "Do you view me as the spiritual leader of our household? If not, what needs to change? If so, tell me how you see that leadership expressed and how it makes you feel when I take leadership."
- "In what ways do you feel that you can trust me in spiritual matters? Where are you having doubts?"
- "Do you think we are honoring God with the way we

spend, give, and save our money? How could we do
better?"

- "What five things do you think we have to do to start
  encouraging our children to own their faith (instead of
  borrowing ours)?"

# Chapter Six

# A Date to Meet My Wife's Need for Emotional Intimacy and Communication

Meg was on the go from the time she woke up each morning: racing the kids to school, working at the library, and maintaining a family calendar. And she was wearing down. Her husband, Joe, missed the long talks they used to have in the earlier years of their marriage. He felt a growing distance between them.

One night as he walked into the house after a long day at work, he saw the droop in Meg's shoulders and made a decision. "Meg, we need some time together. Let's get out of here and have a meal out. I'll call the restaurant and see if our favorite booth beside the fireplace is available. I'll even call the baby-sitter. You take a bit of a breather, and we can leave when the baby-sitter arrives. How about it? I won't take no for an answer." In less than forty minutes they walked out the door.

Alone together for the first time in months, they sat and talked. Joe put his arm around his wife, and she melted. Meg let her thoughts tumble out. "I've been under an inordinate amount of stress at work . . . I'm upset with my sister. . . . It's been a rough day with the kids. . . . I've had a lot of things on my mind, and I don't have a place to take them when we are so busy." He listened as Meg cataloged the stresses she was facing. "Whether it's the kids or the daily stuff, I tend to get anxious and I need someone to download my thoughts with. I miss talking to you," she said, beginning to relax.

"I do too. We've both been too busy lately. How can we change that? I want to spend more time with you."

Two hours later, when the wait staff started to turn off lights in the dining room, Meg and Joe realized that they had reconnected emotionally. They had talked about some solutions to their busyness as well as their jobs, their kids, and their life together.

Taking a deep sigh, Meg looked at her husband and said, "Joe, you knew just what we needed tonight. I feel so much better already. Talking with you always gives me perspective. Thank you for your thoughtfulness. Let's not wait months to do this again."

## The Number Two Love Need of Women

While our survey showed that husbands and wives share four of the five love needs (although they may rank them at a different level of priority), the need for emotional intimacy and communication belongs to wives alone. However, there still is a parallel. Both husbands and wives long for *intimacy*. In fact, both of them place it as their number two love need. But they spell it differently. For women, *intimacy* is spelled T-A-L-K. For men, *intimacy* is spelled S-E-X. So you see, the love need is the same, but the way it needs to be fulfilled is vastly different between men and women.

You guys long for intimacy with your wife in the privacy of your bedroom. You look forward to sex. Your wife does too, but she's going to approach it in an entirely different way.

Let me try to explain this better. Men are able to compartmentalize their lives. You can put all the different parts of your lives in different boxes. You have your friends in a box over there, your daily job in a box on that shelf, your communication with your wife in a box on the other shelf, your sex life with your wife in yet another box, and then your church and community life in another box in the corner. They're all separate boxes. What's happening in one doesn't necessarily affect another one. So you may be exhausted from work, mad at a friend, not in touch with your wife for a particular day, but it takes only one look at her when you get home—and you're ready for sexual involvement. For you, making love is a very separate act from everything else.

Your wife's boxes, however, are all standing in a row, all open, and they have a rope tying them together. Her friends, her daily job, her communication with you, her involvement with the kids, and her sex life with you may be in separate boxes, but they're all closely connected. When one box is affected, there's a chain reaction that affects all the other boxes. So if she's had a rough day at work or with the kids, if she's mad at a friend, or if she feels that she hasn't had much communication or involvement from you during the day, she will feel completely drained. Not even the sight of your muscular build and twinkling eyes can change that. She's not rejecting *you*; it's just that one of her boxes is out of whack, and that is affecting everything else.

## Organizing the Boxes

So how do you step in and meet your wife's need for emotional intimacy and communication? For many men, this is extremely difficult. They don't get it. They shake their heads and decide to not even try. Communication is draining; it can be a challenge. But hey, we're not asking for a whole lot here, guys! We just want to talk—like we used to do back in those dating days.

Let me explain something. Your wife needs sex too. Times of intimacy with you truly are a source of great fulfillment. However, she doesn't ever want to feel as if she is being used. She wants sex with you to come *in the context of* knowing that you love her totally, knowing that she is secure with you. Would you like to know the secret to the greatest sex life ever? Spend some time every day communicating with your wife and meeting her need for emotional intimacy. Trust me on this: you will turn around and find that your wife is much more open to sexual involvement with you when she feels connected to you emotionally.

Now, you may be saying, "Of course I love my wife; she knows that. I told her once back in 1983! That hasn't changed!" Great. I'm glad you still love your wife, but you see, you need to tell her every day. (Three little words; it's easy.) Then you need to help her keep those other boxes in line by being connected to what's going on in her life. You can't solve all of her problems, but when she is out of whack in an area of life, it's going to affect everything else. You would be wise to get in there and help straighten the boxes by listening. As she has a chance to regroup, as she understands that her best friend (you) knows what's going on, then her energy level will come back up, and she will be better able to face the problem. More than that, however, she will feel connected to you when you have listened. That connection will then carry over to her ability and desire to connect with you sexually. You will have met her second most important love need.

## Building Emotional Intimacy: Listening

The key to emotional intimacy is communication with your wife; the key to communication is listening. Your wife needs to know that you hear and value what she says. She doesn't want you to be so drained at the end of your day of listening to everyone else in your life that you have no energy to listen to her. Talking with you is her way of processing her feelings, of getting those boxes back in order. When you truly listen, give her your undivided attention, and try to understand her feelings, you are emotionally connecting with her.

This is not a one-way street. You don't have to just sit and listen. Your wife also wants to hear all about you. If you had an important meeting with a client over lunch, your wife wants to know how it went. Some wives may even want to know what the client looked like, what you had for lunch, and any other small detail you can remember. (Incidentally, that's why you get so much of that kind of detail from her— she enjoys those details. So when she starts giving you all that information, take it in stride and listen. It's just part of her wiring.) You see, your wife has an intense drive to be emotionally transparent with you, and she also wants to know everything about you. When you let her into your world and when you step into her world, you can experience true oneness.

Do you want to earn some big points? Ask your wife what she thinks—get her opinion. Maybe you do this already in the big issues, but get her input on the little things. When she knows you value her opinion, you are touching a deep part of her soul. It may seem small to you guys, but it's big to us!

As you listen to your wife pour out her heart, you need to be careful of what you say. Most of the time your wife does not need you to fix things for her; she needs you to listen and empathize with her. Let me say that in another way. When your wife tells you what upsets her or what makes her discouraged, don't immediately say, "Well, it seems to me that if you would . . ." or "Have you tried . . . ?" Instead, show her understanding. Let her know that you see things from her point of view. Ask how she's dealing with her situation. You can even ask her if she needs your help; then listen to her response. Give her your attention and affection. Hold her as you talk. Give her a shoulder to lean or cry on. When you listen, recognize her emotions and just be there for her as she processes her thoughts and feelings.

At times, of course, this means you're dealing with conflict—some of it directed at you. This means that you need to learn to fight fair, to resolve conflict between the two of you in the most healthy ways possible. (More about this in chapter 4 in *The Five Love Needs of Men and Women* book, where I have given keys that will help, when the two of you need to work through a disagreement.)

When you connect emotionally with your wife, you have found the key to unlock her heart.

## Pre-Date Ideas

Before you consider the suggested dates in each section, ask yourself a few questions:

_ Am I emotionally connected to my wife?
_ Do I really listen to her when she talks and take the time to understand?
_ Is she the most important person in my life? Does she stand head and shoulders above my most important client or customer in my business?
_ Do I show her that she is valuable to me?
_ Have we built walls between us? If so, what can I do to help remove the walls and connect emotionally with my wife?
_ Does she have any unresolved issues that we need to deal with together?

As you consider these questions, you may realize that you haven't connected with your wife for a while. Maybe you haven't really listened to her for a long time. You may have talked, but could you express how she is feeling and what she thinks? You may truly believe that she is the most important person in your life, but does *she* know it? How does she know? How have you shown this? When was the last time you told her how valuable she is to you?

Do you see why you need this date? This is a time for you to truly let your wife know how much she means to you. It's to help you understand that your wife needs this kind of reinforcement every day of your marriage.

## *Four Suggested Dates with Your Wife*

♡ **DATE IDEA #1**
## Your Chick and a Flick
*(Rating: very flexible, easy to plan, low expense)*

Here's a nice, quiet evening at home—not expensive, but certainly lots of fun. You and your wife need to go to the local video store and pick a movie. Tell your wife that she should rent her favorite movie of all time (no matter what it is). If it's a real oldie and the video store doesn't have it, the local library might. Watch the movie with the goal of talking with your wife about why that particular movie is her favorite. If she can't think of a favorite, go to the video store and ask her to pick out some "chick flick" that she wants to see.

Cuddle with your wife while you watch the movie. Try to see it through her eyes. Think of questions you might like to ask her after seeing the movie. Find out how she sees the women in the movie. Are the women portrayed well? Who is her favorite character? Why? Did she like the way the female characters interacted with the males? Did she find the movie romantic? What parts were particularly romantic to her? This then can lead into a time of talking about the Let's Talk questions.

### Prep Steps

○ You don't have to plan way ahead for this one. Be spontaneous. Just make sure your wife knows ahead of time. "Tomorrow night we're going to have a special night

together." Tell her to think about what her favorite movie
is, or to think about a "chick flick" that she's been wanting to see.

○ Go to the video store or library, and check out the tape.

○ Purchase snacks to eat during the movie.

○ If your furniture in the TV room is not great for cuddling,
put a blanket and some pillows on the floor and snuggle
up together.

○ Select the Let's Talk questions you would like to discuss with your wife (write them down or mark them
in this book). Then take along either your list or this
book so that you will remember what you want to talk
about.

Choose an Unforgettable Tip and a Post-Date Idea from the
lists at the end of the chapter.

**DATE IDEA #2**

# A Hot Bath and a Cold Dessert
*(Rating: flexible, easy to plan, low expense)*

Tell your wife you want to give her some time alone to pamper
herself. Take her into the bathroom, where you have placed
some nice smelling bath soaps, lit some candles, and laid out
her favorite nightgown. (Want to score some points? Buy her a
pretty new one.)

Let her indulge in a luxurious bubble bath. If you have children, put them to bed while she is soaking. Then when she has
finished her bath, tell her to come into the bedroom for some
heart-to-heart talking. (You see, she's figuring that you are
expecting something else. But control yourself, guys, this is *her*
love need.) Have a few candles lit and music playing. Have a
nice treat ready to eat together—her favorite ice cream, some
cheesecake, two slices of tiramisu, whatever. Offer her the food,
and then start talking. Use the Let's Talk questions at the end of
the chapter.

### Prep Steps

○ Set aside a night when you and your wife can have quiet time together. She doesn't even need to know—but you *can* give her a hint if you want.

○ Purchase some products she can pamper herself with. Get a loofah, some bubble bath, powder, or whatever looks and smells good. If you want to splurge, purchase a new nightgown for your wife.

○ Buy or prepare the treat you want to share in bed.

○ Purchase candles if you need some.

○ Set everything out in the bathroom for her. Just as you're preparing to put the kids to bed or clean up the dishes, tell her you'll take care of it and send her off to the bathroom. Leave a note there with instructions.

○ While she is soaking, prepare the bedroom with candles, music, and the food.

○ Select the Let's Talk questions you would like to discuss with your wife (write them down or mark them in this book). Then take along either your list or this book so that you will remember what you want to talk about.

Choose an Unforgettable Tip and a Post-Date Idea from the lists at the end of the chapter.

**DATE IDEA #3**

# Out to the Opera (or Something like It)

*(Rating: not flexible, will take some planning, medium to high expense)*

What does your wife really enjoy, but you rarely do because of time or inconvenience? For example, has she wanted to go to the art museum, a particular opera, or a play? Is that a part of her world that the two of you have rarely shared? Then step in.

Plan a day to take her to the museum or an evening to take her to a performance. Plan ahead to get tickets and seating; the

Internet may help you do that. Once you have planned the date, you can just tell your wife you're going out for a very special time. Tell her how to dress, and then take her to the destination. Let it be a surprise!

Plan to go for a meal or dessert, and spend some time talking about what she loves about the opera, the art exhibit, or whatever. This is a way to give her attention and affection as you get into her world and discover more about the intimate parts of her life. Then use some of the Let's Talk questions to explore your wife's inner world more deeply.

### Prep Steps

- ○ Scan the newspaper for ideas about what to see. Have your wife give some input, if needed. If you're planning a museum trip, call to find out the hours it's open.
- ○ Order the tickets, if needed.
- ○ Get the date on both of your schedules—and the family master schedule.
- ○ Schedule a baby-sitter, if needed.
- ○ Tell your wife how to dress.
- ○ If needed, make meal reservations. Or plan on a location for a great dessert and coffee.
- ○ Select the Let's Talk questions you would like to discuss with your wife (write them down or mark them in this book). Then take along either your list or this book so that you will remember what you want to talk about.

Choose an Unforgettable Tip and a Post-Date Idea from the lists at the end of the chapter.

DATE IDEA #4
## Shop Till You Drop
*(Rating: flexible, easy to plan, bring your credit card)*

This one may take a very special kind of guy—but I do actually know some men who enjoy shopping. You're going to take your wife to the place of all places—the mall. Perhaps you know that your wife really needs a new dress for a certain event, or a new outfit for work, or just something fun. Plan an outing together.

Begin your day with breakfast out. Then head for the mall to help her find that perfect outfit. Plan to have some lunch. Then do some "just for fun" shopping—whether it's in a bookstore, a furniture store, or the candle shop. Enjoy just looking and being together.

Take your time with your wife, guys. Be patient. Understand what's going on as she's trying to decide what to buy. You'll learn a lot—and the rewards will be well worth it.

Over one of the meals or at the end of your excursion, take time to talk through the Let's Talk questions.

### Prep Steps

○ Tell your wife ahead of time that you'll be taking her on a date for the day. Pick a time and get it on your calendar.

○ Schedule a baby-sitter, if needed.

○ Wear comfortable shoes. You'll be doing lots of walking.

○ Select the Let's Talk questions you would like to discuss with your wife (write them down or mark them in this book). Then take along either your list or this book so that you will remember what you want to talk about.

Choose an Unforgettable Tip and a Post-Date Idea from the lists below.

~~~

### *Unforgettable Tips*

1. As you talk together, focus entirely on her. Don't allow yourself to be distracted. Look into her eyes, and talk. Let her know that conversing with her is extremely important to you.

2. Ask questions. Dig deep. Let her share her innermost thoughts with you.

3. Reserve judgment or giving solutions. Just listen.
4. Be there for her emotionally. If there are tears, let them come. Don't make her feel embarrassed. Seek to understand and to be there for her.

### Post-Date Ideas

1. Call your wife once each day. Tell her that you just want to hear her voice. And don't forget to say those three little words.
2. Before you crawl out of bed in the morning, cuddle with your wife. Kiss her, give her nonsexual touch, and tell her how much you need her.
3. Set aside a few minutes every day just to talk about your day and hear about your wife's day. Look into her eyes. Give her your attention.
4. Write love notes to your wife. Send them through the mail or e-mail. If you have children, have them deliver the notes. Even if you're in one room of the house, write a love note, seal it in an envelope, and send your child to take it to your wife.
5. Purchase some "pamper yourself" items for your wife, whether or not you do that particular date above. Leave her some nice bubble bath as a gift with a note on it from you saying, "A day without talking to you would burst my bubble." On another day, leave a nice candle with a note that says, "Coming home to talk to you brightens my day." You get the idea.

### Let's Talk

Choose some questions/comments from each level to help guide your discussion during your date. This way you can learn more about how you can meet your wife's need for emotional intimacy and communication.

**LEVEL 1:**

## Dip Your Toes into the Water

- "Who are your heroes or people you've looked up to over the years?"
- "What really gets on your nerves?"
- "Are you generally an optimist or a pessimist? How do you feel about that?"
- "How can I connect to you more deeply?"
- "Do I touch you enough? In what ways would you like me to physically show my love for you in public? Holding hands, putting my arm around your waist or shoulder?"
- "When you are struggling with a problem area, how would you like me to respond?"

**LEVEL 2:**

## Up to Your Ankles

- "What issues do we seem to have trouble discussing? Why are these difficult, and what should we do to help us communicate about them?"
- "What can we do to grab fifteen minutes a day of uninterrupted talk when we're both awake enough to pay attention?"
- "In what ways can I continue to 'court' you the way I did when we were dating?"
- "How well did your parents communicate? Was one 'the talker' and the other more quiet?" Then talk about your parents. Consider how your families have affected your current method of communication in your marriage.
- "Does it ever seem that I'm not giving you my full attention when you're talking to me? What do I need to do to show you that I am paying attention?"

**LEVEL 3:**

## Treading in Deeper Waters

- "Do I ever give you the silent treatment? If so, how do you feel when I do this? How might we break this pattern?"

- "When we have a fight or an intense discussion, does it seem like I'm really listening to what you say, or am I more interested in getting in what I want to say? What signal can I give to let you know I'm listening and understanding what you're saying?"
- "If I was to write more notes to you, what kinds of things would you like the notes to say?"
- "What item in our schedule would you most like to change?"
- "How can we set the right atmosphere in our marriage so that both of us feel safe sharing secrets and feelings with each other?"

**LEVEL 4:**

*Bouncing on the Waves*

- "What do you think 'marital intimacy' means?"
- "How would you characterize the level of honesty in our relationship?" (Let your wife choose one or more of the following statements to describe how she thinks you handle honesty and the truth. Your wife's response will reveal how secure she feels with you. If you disagree with her assessment, ask her to give you examples of times you have not been honest with her. This is a time to gain information, not to argue.)
  1. Don't ask, don't tell.
  2. You are totally honest about the small stuff.
  3. You are totally honest about everything.
  4. You know I hide a few things, but you deal with this approach better than knowing all the truth.
  5. You're afraid to tell me some things sometimes for fear of how I'll respond.
  6. You don't talk because you feel that I can't handle the truth.
  7. Other.

- "In what three ways can I become a better listener?"
- "When do you feel the most distant from me? Does that

feeling cause you to want to draw closer, move further away, or stay where you are until the feeling goes away?"

- "What emotions do you have the most trouble dealing with? Do I trigger these emotions in you? If yes, how can I avoid that? If no, how can I help you with your emotional struggle?"
- "What are some of the most important lessons about life you've learned this past year?"

**LEVEL 5:**

## Diving in Head First

- "What do you think is the difference between emotional intimacy and physical intimacy? Which do we share more of? Which do you need more of? How can I help to meet that need better?"
- "How do we deal with our anger at each other? When have we let the sun go down on our anger? How can we work through our difficulties in a more God-honoring way?"
- "What are some ways the world is trying to separate us in our marriage relationship?"
- "Do you ever feel that I'm more 'at one' with my job, the kids, or a hobby than I am with you? What makes you feel that way? How can I be more 'at one' with you?"
- "Do you ever wonder if we will not go the distance in our marriage? How can I improve in how I serve you? In what ways could our marriage become stronger and more secure so that you are not tempted to think about not finishing together?"

# ~ *Chapter Seven* ~

# A Date to Meet My Wife's Need for Unconditional Love and Acceptance

Tom saw the rising frustration in Kathryn. She'd been gone a lot during the past week, and their apartment was a mess. The sink was full of dishes, and laundry was scattered all over the place. When Tom mumbled something about not having clean socks, Kathryn lost it.

When she opened her mouth, she unleashed all of her frustration on Tom. He was stunned.

After Kathryn settled down, she was anguished about her outburst—not her first in their three-year marriage. "Tom, I'm so sorry I beat you up with my words. I wish I could take them back. I'm so ashamed of myself."

"Kathryn, I forgive you for yelling at me." And before he said anything else—anything about the pace she'd been keeping by taking care of everyone else's needs and ignoring her own—he asked himself a few questions: *Do I really know what Kathryn's life is like, all day every day? Do I understand how much stress she is handling?*

Gathering his thoughts, he said, "Kathryn, you don't have to bear the brunt of this place. Let's talk through what needs to get done, and we will do it together. I love you, and I don't want you to feel overwhelmed."

Kathryn knows unconditional love. She has experienced Christlike love from Tom, a love that looks beyond what has happened and seeks to love her through her failures. And in the security of that love, she later was able to talk to Tom about her anger, confessing again and discussing better ways to handle her frustration.

When Kathryn and Tom shared the blow-up incident with their small-group Bible study a few weeks later, she turned to her husband and said, "I know I am loved for several reasons. Tom tells me throughout the day and shows me in all sorts of ways. He loves me even when I am unlovable. He loves me even when it would be easier to be angry with me and walk away. I am so thankful to God for Tom. He motivates me to want to love him with the same kind of love."

## The Number One Love Need of Women

Every wife shares the need for unconditional love and acceptance—the need to be loved when she is unlovable. In our survey, this was, in fact, the number one need of a majority of our female respondents.

As a wife, I know how much it means to know that Gary loves me unconditionally. I know that you love your wife. But what does it mean to love her unconditionally? Well, unconditional love is just that—love without conditions. In other words, you don't love your wife only when she looks good or she lands a promotion or she loses some weight or when the house is clean. You love her without those conditions. When you do that, you are loving unconditionally.

Unconditional love is love that we need the most when we deserve it the least. It's the kind of love that reaches out even after we have said something hurtful or when we know we've made poor choices and have clearly blown it. It's the kind of love that knows how to say something tenderly and knows when not to say a word. It's the kind of love that remains committed even when we say and do ugly things. Unconditional love is a redemptive love that pursues us when we act in unholy ways and that motivates us to do things we are not capable of doing on our own.

In marriage, a couple's unconditional love for each other comes out of God's unconditional love for us as individuals. This pursuing love promises to love, protect, and care for us forever. The perfect picture of unconditional love is Christ's death for us "while we were still sinners" (Romans 5:8). He loves us even though we struggle and battle with selfishness, pride, and any number of other sins that keep us from loving well.

This is the kind of love your wife needs from you. It's a tall order, I know, but remember that no one expects you to do it alone. In fact, you can't. It is a supernatural love, found in the very nature of God. That's why you have to lean on God's strength to receive that love. When you know you're not up to the task or feel out of control, ask God to help you. Think about what it feels like to be the recipient of lavish love from God and then give that love to your wife.

Unconditional love has the power to change ordinary men and women into extraordinary people. And it reaps enormous rewards. When you love unconditionally, you set the tone for your wife to love you unconditionally in return.

Your wife isn't perfect. Remember, you are the one person who sees that most clearly. You are the one person who sees all her faults and fears. In a sense, that could give you a whole lot of power over her. I hope you don't see it that way. But think about it: what do you do with what you know about your wife? Do you tease her with hurtful words? Worse, do you tease her with hurtful words in front of others? Do you put her down? Do you withhold your love until she corrects those faults? If you answer yes to any of these questions, you are loving conditionally and you are creating a huge fault line in your relationship—a fault line that can at any moment open up and destroy your marriage.

Sadly, when a woman feels loved *conditionally,* she feels pressure to perform in certain ways, to look and act a certain way. If she senses that your love is based on her performance, how much she earns, appearances, or success, her sense of worth will vacillate. She will be preoccupied with thinking, *Am I doing everything just right? Am I what my husband needs today? Am I performing well?* Of course, she will know that she cannot truly be herself—with her faults, her fears, her worries, her needs—because your love fluctuates with the degree of approval you give her.

When a woman is loved lavishly, she is free to be who she is because she feels secure in knowing that you love her—no matter what. When you encourage your wife to be herself, you help her gain freedom from the pressure to gain people's approval.

I hope that the richness of your life together allows you to see faults in your wife and love her through them. I hope that you cover them with your love. Your wife needs to know that you love her during times of pain and failure. She needs your tenderness. Show her that you love her no matter what. Love her the way God loves her. Become "God with skin on" to your wife.

Unconditional love can transform your wife.

Unconditional love can transform your marriage.

## Willing to Love Unconditionally

Have you seen the movie *My Fair Lady*? Perhaps you agreed when you heard Professor Henry Higgins ask the age-old question, "Why can't a woman be more like a man?"

Men and women are different. God made them that way. A woman's need for unconditional love can express itself in ways that are different from a man's need for the same thing. Just because you and your wife have the same need doesn't mean that it can be met in the same way.

Remember, your wife is a woman.

Women need their husbands to show them unconditional love at their point of pain, their point of vulnerability, and their point of mistakes or failure. Let's talk about that briefly. (For a fuller discussion, see chapter 2 of *The Five Love Needs of Men and Women*.)

You need to be willing to love your wife in her pain, love her where she is most vulnerable, and love her when she fails. She needs to know that she can come to you and express her hurt or frustration—and that you will genuinely listen and—this is important—*not try to solve her problem*.

Did you hear that? Now you may be thinking, *Who in his (that is, her) right mind doesn't want to hear my logical solution to the problem?* The answer: your wife. At least she doesn't want to hear it right away. Instead, when she talks about her pain due to disappointment or unmet expectations, she wants you to make an *emotional* connection with her. This is your time to shine and show her you can connect. Remember that when they are under stress, men talk silently and women process out loud. Give your wife some time, and she might indeed want your advice, but at first, she just wants you to *listen*. Wrap your arms around her and hold her. You are her advocate—now's the time to show her. Chances are she's being hard enough on herself, and she knows what she should have done. It's not your responsibility to tell her what she should have or could have done. And never use her failure against her—never.

## Showing Unconditional Love

Now you know when your wife needs unconditional love, so it's time for learning *how* she needs to experience that love.

Your wife needs encouragement daily (don't you too?). Tell

her you love her and will never leave her. Let her know that you are with her. Spend time with her. Compliment her. Tell her she is all the woman you ever need. Respect her opinion. Set aside time every day to talk—you tell about your day, and make sure she tells about hers. Be tender with her when she faces hormonal changes. Serve her by looking for ways to lighten her load.

## Pre-Date Ideas

Before you consider the suggested dates, take a moment and think about the woman you married. Close your eyes, and ask yourself:

_ Do I really know what my wife's day is like, all day every day?

_ How much stress does she face? (No fair comparing hers with yours.)

_ How do I treat her when I am home?

_ What would our friends say about how I treat my wife? What would our kids say about how I treat their mother?

_ Is she presently facing any fear, anxiety, or worry? Do I know why?

_ Has she hurt or failed me? How have I dealt with it?

_ Do I show her unconditional love?

   If your wife is wrapped up in anxiety or if she is cranky or if she knows she has hurt you—*she desperately needs your unconditional love*. Does this come naturally for any of us? No. The last thing you may feel like doing is showing love to your wife—and yet that is why it is the first thing you must do to compel your love to go to a deeper level. Who doesn't want a soul mate to walk with through difficult times? Such times don't have to be a wedge driving you apart but can actually be a gift used as a catalyst to drive you closer together as a couple into the very arms of Christ.

   If today things are pretty smooth with your wife, then your

job is easier. But often when the marriage is on a smooth part of the road, we simply forget that the need is still there—until you hit a bump in the road. It lightens the load when you call your wife from work. It refreshes her when you chat about how her day is going. Ask what you can do to help (pick up something on the way home, perhaps?). Remind her of how much you appreciate her loveliness. Compliment her—about her clothes, her organizational skills, her handling of the kids, her ability to do her job *and* be a great wife and mother, whatever. Carving out even a few minutes a day to spend time with her—a few minutes when you can talk, reconnect—lets her know she is the most important person in the world to you.

Consider the Date Ideas below. You may need to tweak them to fit you and your wife. Don't forget to bring along with you the Let's Talk questions.

Finally, look over the Unforgettable Tips and the Post-Date Ideas that are included after the four Date Ideas. Choose one from each list—or make up your own.

*Four Suggested Dates with Your Wife*

### ♡ DATE IDEA #1
## A Long Drive Together
*(Rating: very flexible, easy to prepare, low expense)*

Take a long walk or drive. If you walk, go somewhere you won't run into people you know. If you drive, preferably head out to a rural road where you won't deal with traffic. This is a time of communicating together, but it is not so threatening because you're not sitting and facing each other. Open up some snacks and drinks, and get talking. If you come across something fun or interesting (a roadside stand, an antique shop) and your wife says, "Oooh," then stop and check it out! Resist the impulse if it's something you like but she doesn't— this date is for *her*, remember?

If your car allows, have your wife sit right next to you. If not, find a way to hold hands as much as possible. If you're walking, hold hands and walk as close to one another as possible. The physical connection will draw you closer and make it easier to talk. This is a quiet time for you to focus on her and to show her your unconditional love by doing lots of listening as you talk through your questions.

### Prep Steps

○ Get the date on both of your schedules—and the family master schedule.

○ Schedule a baby-sitter, if needed.

○ If you're going for a drive, clean out the car and make sure it has gas (unless, of course, you want to run out of gas on a deserted country road . . .).

○ Tell your wife to dress comfortably and casually (believe me, she wants to know what to wear). If you're going for a long walk, tell her to wear her walking shoes and to bring along a sweater or sweatshirt.

○ Tell her it will be just the two of you—no one else around to see you.

○ Stop and get a snack to munch on in the car as you drive or carry as you walk—some kind of treat you both love to share. Also get something to drink.

○ Select the Let's Talk questions you would like to discuss with your wife (write them down or mark them in this book). Then take along either your list or this book so that you will remember what you want to talk about.

Choose an Unforgettable Tip and a Post-Date Idea from the lists at the end of the chapter.

**DATE IDEA #2**

# A Place of Healing

*(Rating: very flexible, easy to prepare—you'll just need to think about how to do it best, low expense)*

Has your wife been through a tough time lately? Has your marriage been suffering? Does your wife know that you love her no matter what? What challenges your ability to love her unconditionally?

- Has she failed at something important to her that has affected her self-esteem? Has this, in turn, affected your marriage?
- Has there been a betrayal, a huge disappointment, or even infidelity? Perhaps this occurred in the past, but it is still casting a looming shadow over your marriage.
- Have you been so involved in your work and other activities that you and your wife are feeling distant and at odds?

No matter what kind of hurt or disappointment you're experiencing, your wife needs to know of your unconditional love. When you say to her, "I love you no matter what," both you and she need to know what that "what" is. You need to be able to say to her, "Of course I love you, no matter what!" or "I love you and forgive you for past mistakes," or "I know I've not been very attentive lately, and I want to tell you how much I love you."

Identify one of these situations that needs healing and reconciliation. Then arrange a date around that situation. Can you do something to help her process more completely in order to help her experience freedom in an area of captivity? You might take your wife back to a place of hurt, anxiety, or failure, and in that location offer unconditional love that can heal and restore. For example, if your wife feels like a failure because she didn't get that promotion at work, drive to the parking lot of her office building for a time of discussion. Tell her that you love her "no matter what." If she has betrayed you (either emotionally or physically), take her to a quiet place—a park or even an empty chapel—and speak words of recommitment and healing to her. If she is suffering a debilitating loss (of health, a friend, a child, a family member), go to a place that reminds her of a positive memory with that person or a time when she had full health. Tell her that you love her "no matter what."

Perhaps you realize that you have not shown your wife unconditional love for a long time. Maybe you've been critical or too caught up in your own activities. Go to a place that represents your love (think about it—be creative!) and speak words of commitment to her. For example, if you've been paying more attention to your work than to your wife, spend some time in the parking lot of *your* office building. Confess to your wife that you have not been loving her as you should and that you want to commit to loving her better now.

You can use the Let's Talk questions in any location. Your desire for this date is that your wife will know beyond a doubt that you love her "no matter what." This security will help your wife to recover, to heal, and then to soar on into life, buoyed by your support and love. Guys, trust me on this, you won't believe what a talk like this can do for a hurting wife! Unconditional love has an amazing ability to heal all kinds of hurts.

### Prep Steps

○ Get the date on both of your schedules—and the family master schedule.

○ Schedule a baby-sitter, if needed.

○ Tell your wife to dress casually—that you're just going for a drive and conversation.

○ Think about where you want to go. What location will be most meaningful so that she understands the connection? What location will allow for conversation alone together to talk through the issue at hand?

○ Buy your wife one long-stemmed red rose. Give it to her as you get in the car.

○ Select the Let's Talk questions you would like to discuss with your wife (write them down or mark them in this

book). Then take along either your list or this book so that you will remember what you want to talk about.

Choose an Unforgettable Tip and a Post-Date Idea from the lists at the end of the chapter.

**DATE IDEA #3**

## That "Special Place"
*(Rating: This will vary depending on where that "special place" is.)*

Do you have a favorite place where the two of you have been in the past? Do you still live near the location where you had your first date? (If you remember, you're already earning points!) How about the place where you asked your wife to marry you? Make arrangements to go there.

Depending on where this place is, you may need to make further arrangements in order to have a quiet place to talk about some of the discussion questions. A quiet restaurant is one thing; however, if your first date was in a noisy place with a band or at a baseball game, then plan to go to a quiet location afterward so you can talk. Your unconditional love will shine through to your wife as she sees your careful thought in this date and your desire to relive special moments with her. Your desire to spend time with her in a special place will reinforce to her your unconditional love.

### Prep Steps
○ Get the date on both of your schedules—and the family master schedule.

○ Schedule a baby-sitter, if needed.

○ Tell your wife to dress appropriately depending on where you are going. Realize that it is very important to her not to feel over- or underdressed. If she has an outfit that you love to see her wear, then ask her to wear it if it works for this occasion.

○ Buy your wife a piece of jewelry—it need not be extravagant or expensive. After all, perhaps you gave her a ring in this location; now give her a pair of earrings or a necklace.

○ Make reservations, if required. If you're going to a restaurant, try to get the same table you sat at before.

○ Select the Let's Talk questions you would like to discuss with your wife (write them down or mark them in this book). Then take along either your list or this book so that you will remember what you want to talk about.

Choose an Unforgettable Tip and a Post-Date Idea from the lists at the end of the chapter.

**DATE IDEA #4**
# Make a Dream Come True
*(Rating: probably not very flexible, will take research and planning, may be expensive)*

Okay, now let's be a bit extravagant. Do something over and above. Maybe your wife has said she always wanted to ride in a hot-air balloon. Do some research and plan a ride in a hot-air balloon. Maybe she's always wanted to dine in that ritzy French restaurant in the city. Make reservations.

Think back, and see if you can remember something your wife has said that she has always wanted to do—or just surreptitiously ask her. She doesn't need to know she's actually going to get to do it (depending on reality of course—a trip to the space station is still quite expensive!). The point is to show your wife you love her so much that you want to make one of her dreams come true.

## Prep Steps

○ Get the date on both of your schedules—and the family master schedule.

○ Schedule a baby-sitter, if needed.

○ Tell your wife how she needs to dress for this particular outing.

○ Make the required reservations.

○ Buy some fun kind of clue to leave for her on the day of the date. For example, if you're going ballooning, tape a balloon to the bathroom mirror.

○ Select the Let's Talk questions you would like to discuss with your wife (write them down or mark them in this book). Then take along either your list or this book so that you will remember what you want to talk about.

Choose an Unforgettable Tip and a Post-Date Idea from the lists below.

~ ~ ~

## Unforgettable Tips

1. At some point on the date—you'll know when it feels right—turn to your wife, take both of her hands in yours, look straight into her eyes, and tell her you love her "for better or worse, richer or poorer, in sickness and in health, so long as we both shall live." Then kiss her.

2. Buy your wife a special gift. Think about something you know she likes but would not buy for herself. It can be simple or small—it's the thought that counts.

3. Ask your wife to give you her engagement and wedding rings. Take them to a jeweler to be checked, cleaned, and polished. Ask the jeweler to put them in a pretty box. The night of the date, present them again to your wife. Tell her you'd marry her all over again.

4. If appropriate, have a limousine pick you up at home and take you to your location.

## Post-Date Ideas

1. Leave a note where your wife can see it at some point the next day, telling her that you love her.

2. Get across the point that you love her with all your heart by buying a heart-shaped box of chocolates or a big heart-shaped cookie.
3. Order flowers and have them sent to her workplace, or schedule them to arrive at home when she's there but you're not.
4. Begin to act on at least one comment that she made during the date. Show her that you listened and that you care to meet her need for unconditional love.
5. Mail her a card—funny, sexy, profound, whatever. Write a note telling her that you had a wonderful time on your date with her and you would like to go out with her again.

### Let's Talk

Choose some questions/comments from each level to help guide your discussion during your date. This way you can learn more about how you can meet your wife's need for unconditional love and acceptance.

**LEVEL 1:**

### Dip Your Toes into the Water

- "What was your day like today? What are the stresses you have been feeling in the past few months?"
- "I want you to know that I really appreciate you because . . ."
- "Do you feel secure about your role in life? If not, how can I help?"
- "What does the term *unconditional love* mean to you? How can I show you that I love you unconditionally? What can I do better?"
- "Do I act as if your opinions are important? If not, what can I do better to show you that I value what you think and I take your words seriously?"

**LEVEL 2:**

### Up to Your Ankles

- "Do I say 'I love you' often enough? If not, how often

would you like me to say it to you? When? Tell me what it means to you when I say these three little words."

- Make a list of five things that you have always been able to count on your wife for, read that list to her, and thank her.
- "What are the top five ways I can give you a tangible expression of my love?"
- "In general, how do you feel about yourself? How can I help you feel more confident (secure, hopeful, whatever)?"
- "When we are with our friends, what can I do to show them that I love you?"

### LEVEL 3:
*Treading in Deeper Waters*

- "Do I hug and kiss you enough? If not, how often do you want me to hug and kiss you? Tell me what it means to you when I do this."
- Ask your wife to complete this sentence: "When I'm at the worst time in my hormonal cycle, the best things you can do are . . ."
- "Do you ever sense that I sometimes put conditions on my love for you? If so, what are the conditions that you feel I am placing on you? When do you feel the most insecure about my love?"
- Tell your wife at least five areas where your love for her has deepened since you've been married.
- Ask your wife to complete this sentence: "I would feel safer sharing my feelings with you if . . ."
- "Am I consistent in matching my loving words toward you with loving behavior?"

### LEVEL 4:
*Bouncing on the Waves*

- Ask your wife to complete one or more of the following questions/sentences:
    1. "Would you love me even if I . . . ?"
    2. "I need your love especially when I . . ."

3. "I sometimes feel that I don't deserve your love
because . . ."
4. "You would never love me if you knew . . ."
Respond to her statement(s) with loving words and
gestures that will make your wife feel secure in your love.

- "Is there any emotional baggage we've brought into this
  marriage that needs to be unpacked? Do you think this
  process requires professional help, or can we handle it
  ourselves? How can I help in the healing process?"
- "What three things do I do for you that really make you
  feel like the woman of my dreams? What would you like
  me to do?"
- "When I disagree with you, how can I best communicate
  that without making you feel put down?"
- "Do you have worries about our marriage? What are they?
  How can we deal with these together?"
- "God loves us unconditionally. How can I show you the
  same kind of unconditional love? Where do you most need
  to see that in our relationship?"

**LEVEL 5:**

*Diving in Head First*

- "Have I ever broken your heart? If so, when? How could I
  have handled that situation differently? What can I do to
  heal that situation?"
- "Have I ever made you feel devalued?" If she says yes, ask
  her to explain the circumstance and how she felt. Don't try
  to justify yourself. Hear what she felt. Ask for her forgiveness. Say, "I would like to show that I value you. What
  behavior would help you feel valued?"
- If your wife has been unfaithful to you (either emotionally
  or physically), say, "I want you to know that I forgive you
  for [whatever the circumstances were]. I'm sorry that I
  contributed to that situation by [whatever you feel was
  your part]. How can I help you feel so secure in my love

that you will never look beyond our marriage for satisfaction?"

- If you have ever been unfaithful to your wife (and she knows about it), say, "I am sorry that I violated our relationship. I ask you to forgive me again. I want to commit myself to becoming the husband you need me to be by learning to meet your needs. What is the next step you need me to take?"
- "How can we affair-proof our marriage?"
- "How can we divorce-proof our marriage?"

# Part Three

# A Wife Plans Dates for Her Husband

*~Chapter Eight~*

# A Date to Meet My Husband's Need for Spiritual Intimacy

"I really want to be the servant leader of our home and spiritually stir Ellen, but it is a tough call for me, Gary," Brent shared. "I just feel like I come up short. Recently I made it a priority to get serious about my time in the Bible. The rewards have been remarkable as I see God's design for me throughout the Scripture. My prayer life is getting better, but it is still hard for me to initiate prayer with Ellen and the kids. It seems that when I do initiate it, Ellen only wants more, which leaves me feeling a little inadequate and fearful that I won't be able to deliver all I need to. It's a real tension for me, knowing the results and the promises of God yet also realizing my inadequacy."

"Brent, if Ellen were here and you could tell her what you needed from her, what would you say to her?" I probed.

"Good question. It really helps when I know she is praying for me. It also helps when she affirms what I *do* and is quieter about what I *haven't* done. I grow a lot through her encouragement, but I'm discouraged when I try to measure up to an expressed or unspoken level of spiritual leadership."

Brent's comments sum up what a lot of guys experience. They want to connect spiritually with their wives, but they feel a

little inadequate in doing so. As you read earlier in this book,
Barb came to Christ before I did. Her relationship with Jesus
Christ was incredibly alluring to me. It has only become more
so over the years. Earlier in our marriage I was somewhat intim-
idated by her growth and love affair with the Lord, but over
time I realized that my insecurity and fear was that I could never
*lead* her if I was comparing my spiritual life with hers. I needed
to shift my viewpoint and pursue God in my own way. When I
finally got on that track, my spiritual relationship began to soar,
and Barb's response did too. When she encourages me in the
Word, shares with me what she is learning in prayer, or
discusses spiritual matters with me, I am stirred spiritually. As
Barb points out my spiritual growth, study of the Bible, and
spiritual insights, I feel encouraged to grow more.

## The Number Five Love Need of Men

In our survey, both men and women responded with "spiritual
intimacy" among their top five love needs. For women, this
need came in at number three; for men, it is number five.
Clearly, spiritual connection is vital in a Christian marriage—
and both husband and wife long for it.

However, as we are learning with the other love needs, just
because both husband and wife have the same desire doesn't
mean that the desire can be fulfilled in the same way. Wives,
the way that your love need for spiritual connection and intimacy should be met is very different from the way that you
need to meet that same love need for your husband.

We're just different (as if you didn't know that already!).

And I need to tell you that we guys really struggle with this
one. It doesn't come easily. You see, as Christian men, we
understand that we need to be growing spiritually. We need to
have a spiritual connection with God, with you, and with
other believers.

But there's another whole dimension to this. We also know

that God has made us the spiritual leaders in our marriages and in our homes. We see that as both a privilege and a responsibility. We are honored with such a high calling, yet we often are frustrated because of what it demands of us. We know that we need to be servant leaders, and yet sometimes our own lives get in the way and we feel that we are letting you down. Being a spiritual leader, to us, means being "on" all the time—always wise, always fearless, and always trusting in God. And you know as well as we do that we often fall short of that goal.

That's why we need you to connect with us. That's why we need you to help meet our love need for spiritual intimacy.

## Working to Make the Connection

Your husband may be trying to be the spiritual leader in your home, and if he is making attempts, you need to applaud and encourage him. As I already mentioned, spiritual leadership is hard for us. We're trying to figure it out as we go along—walking that tightrope of servant leadership. We know we are the **spiritual** head of the family, yet we don't want to put you down in any way. We see our position of leadership, but we're not sure how to accept and honor it.

This is where you come in. This is where we need your help. We don't need you to play Junior Holy Spirit in our lives—telling us what we should be doing. We do, however, need to sense your support behind us, your desire for us to take the leadership, and your willingness to honor us as we do so.

We need to be grounded in four basic areas in order for us to be the leaders God wants us to be.

*We need to have personal time in God's Word.* We need you to reinforce us in this. Give us opportunity to have devotional time alone. Pray for us to have a thirst for the Scriptures. Share with us what you are learning in your devotional time. Even purchase materials that you think we might be interested in using in our personal studies.

*We also need to have consistent times of prayer.* It might surprise you to know that this is a difficult area for many men. Oh, we may pray, but we may have a hard time with shallowness and inconsistency. Pray for us to deepen our prayer lives. Ask us to pray for you—and give us specifics. Tell us what we can pray about for our children.

*We need fellowship and worship.* We need to be involved in a local church, worshiping and fellowshiping with other believers. If you and your husband are not currently in a church, you need to work together to find a strong Bible-teaching church. Talk about joining a small group with other believers.

*Finally, we need spiritual intimacy with you and with our kids.* Let us know that you are open to reading the Bible and praying together. Ask us to tell you what we're reading and learning in our devotional times. If you've had to step in and take the leadership by default, let God give you the grace to step back so that we can step in. Help make it easy for us. Get a devotional book we can read at dinnertime and discuss with the family.

In short, many men long for this kind of intimacy but don't quite know how to make it work in their marriages and in their families. That's where you and your husband, working together, can make it happen.

## When It Doesn't Come Easily

But suppose your husband is lacking in this area of spiritual leadership in the home. Then what? Perhaps he fits one of these descriptions:

Some guys don't get it. They just don't understand that they are supposed to have a spiritual relationship with you—they might not even consider this to be one of their love needs. They didn't grow up in a Christian family, or they didn't see this type of spiritual leadership displayed in their families as they were growing up. While you don't need to force this love need on him, it is also very clear that a Christian marriage is really a relationship of three: God, your husband, and you. If your husband's spiritual connection isn't in place, your relationship suffers. You wives can be a great help by gently showing the value you place on our relationship with God.

Some guys get it, but they're inconsistent in acting on it. They get what I call "spiritual hiccups." They may have a tendency to drift away when life gets busy or stressful. The good thing, however, is that these guys often will sense that something is wrong, and then they'll get themselves back on track. You wives can be a great help to your husband here as well by gently prodding him back on the right track.

Still other guys get it, but they don't want it. Something is going on deep inside their hearts, and it's causing them to rebel spiritually. They may be running from God in shame or guilt. The good thing here is that at some point God will chase them down and bring them back to himself. What you wives have been doing in the meantime, however, will be invaluable—and that is continuing to love us and pray for us.

Remember, however, that your goal should not be to change your husband—to make him conform to the standard of spiritual leadership that you have in your mind for the "perfect" husband. You won't change us—and nagging at us is not going to help. Trust me. The only person you can change is you. If your husband is ignorant of what to do, is drifting, or is rebelling, what can you do? You can keep pursuing your personal relationship with God, and you can pray faithfully for your husband. Be patient. Let God work in your husband's life. Don't give up. Ever.

## Pre-Date Ideas

Before you consider the suggested dates in this section, I'd like you to think about your husband for a few minutes. Focus on the following questions:

_ How would I describe my husband's personal relationship

with Jesus Christ? What makes my husband tick spiritually?

_ Does my husband have a daily devotional time? When? Does he pray consistently, or is it a struggle?

_ In what ways has he taken the spiritual leadership in our household?

_ Do I nag my husband about this? If so, how is he reacting?

_ Do I pray for my husband? How often? What am I praying about? What should I be praying about?

If you're fortunate enough to have a husband who readily takes leadership and who hungrily pursues his relationship with God, then thank God for him right now. Ask God what you can do to be more supportive and encouraging to your husband as he continues to grow spiritually.

If your husband is not having an easy time of this, then you need to continue to love and support your husband anyway. Don't withhold your love or refuse to meet his other love needs just because he's floundering in this area. You'll only exacerbate the problem if you nag, get angry, or compare him to other men. Continue to love him and pray for him. Continue to grow spiritually yourself. Let God work in your husband's life. As you pray, be patient. God promises to answer.

*Four Suggested Dates with Your Husband*

### DATE IDEA #1
# Personal Worship Connection
*(Rating: flexible, fairly easy to prepare, probably low expense)*

Ask your husband, "Where is the place that you feel closest to God?" He may have to think about it, or he may have an immediate answer. For this date, take him to that place.

He may tell you some place in nature—such as the mountains or near the ocean (and you may have to be creative if you

don't happen to live near these at present!). If you are like us
and live in the Midwest, he may choose a drive in the country
or time talking on a special park bench. The point is to
discover the place where he senses God's presence. Then you
take him there.

While you're there together, snuggle close and ask him why
this location means so much to him spiritually. During your
time there, discuss your Let's Talk questions.

### Prep Steps

○ Ask your husband about the location where he feels closest to God.

○ Make plans to go to this location. Choose a date that is
workable and put it on everyone's schedule.

○ Plan for a baby-sitter, if needed.

○ Take along anything you might need. For example, if
you're going to sit on the beach, take a blanket. If it's
going to get cool, make sure you both have sweatshirts.
And don't forget his favorite treat for refreshment.

○ Select the Let's Talk questions you would like to discuss
with your husband (write them down or mark them in
this book). Then take along either your list or this
book so that you will remember what you want to talk
about.

Choose an Unforgettable Tip and a Post-Date Idea from the
lists at the end of the chapter.

**DATE IDEA #2**
## All's Quiet
*(Rating: flexible, easy to prepare, low expense)*

In order to have time to talk about spiritual things, consider
taking your husband to a quiet chapel or a park. It may be that
he can't think of a particular place where he feels closest to
God (as suggested in Date #1), so you can help him out.

Perhaps there is a small chapel in one of the bigger churches in your town (you don't necessarily have to go to your own church). Find one that is open during a time when you should be able to have it to yourself. Even the big open sanctuary of a church with stained glass windows on a sunny afternoon can be a very inspirational setting.

Take your husband to this location and sit quietly for a while. Then you can use your Let's Talk questions to begin your discussion about your husband's need for spiritual connection.

### Prep Steps

○ Do a little research and find a quiet chapel or empty church that you can visit sometime during the week when it will be empty of other activities.

○ Plan the date with your husband and get it on your schedules.

○ Schedule a baby-sitter, if needed.

○ Select the Let's Talk questions you would like to discuss with your husband (write them down or mark them in this book). Then take along either your list or this book so that you will remember what you want to talk about.

Choose an Unforgettable Tip and a Post-Date Idea from the lists at the end of the chapter.

DATE IDEA #3
# The Great Outdoors
*(Rating: flexible, easy to prepare, low expense)*

There's nothing much better than the great outdoors to feel closeness to God. If your husband is an outdoorsman, then he probably will love a date where you take him to his favorite outdoor place. Maybe this date will take the form of a hike in the mountains. Maybe you'll end up in a canoe on the lake. Make sure it's an activity that will allow you to talk (cross-country skiing should be saved for another time!).

Go to this location and plan to spend a few hours just relaxing. Use the quiet time to discuss the Let's Talk questions.

## Prep Steps

○ Choose an outdoor location where you know your husband will enjoy a favorite activity such as hiking or boating.

○ Choose a time to do this and get it on your schedules. Since this is a "weather permitting" date, you may need to be a bit more spontaneous (depending on the weather report) and flexible (in case the weather report is wrong!).

○ Schedule a baby-sitter, if needed.

○ Take along any gear appropriate for the activity.

○ You'll probably want some snacks wherever you go, so pack some goodies.

○ Select the Let's Talk questions you would like to discuss with your husband (write them down or mark them in this book). Then take along either your list or this book so that you will remember what you want to talk about.

Choose an Unforgettable Tip and a Post-Date Idea from the lists at the end of the chapter.

**DATE IDEA #4**

# Road Trip

*(Rating: flexible, will take research and planning, medium to high expense)*

Are you ready for a road trip? You're going to plan an unforgettable day away for your husband. This will be a road trip/spiritual retreat for both of you.

You'll plan your day based on your study of a map of nearby towns. Target some locations to visit and make a big circle from home in the morning and then back in the evening. Explore each location. For example, at your first stop, find a coffeeshop for an early morning snack. Next location, find a restaurant and have brunch. Next location, do some shopping (for something for *him,* this is *his* date, remember? If it's a hardware store—then it's a hardware store!). Next stop, lunch. And so on.

The key to this date is that there should be some driving time between each location (at least twenty minutes). During the time in the car, you'll discuss the Let's Talk questions. Being away, undistracted by the normal routine, and alone together will give you ample opportunity to dig into your husband's soul. In addition, the stops here and there can lighten things up a bit and give you an opportunity to enjoy each other in new settings.

### Prep Steps

○ Get a map, and trace a workable route for a day trip in your local environs. Watch the mileage, and plan accordingly.

○ If you know of fun restaurants, bakeries, or stores in some of those towns, plan to stop at those. If the places are completely unknown, enjoy the adventure of seeing what you can find together. Some of the best restaurants, for example, are the little hole-in-the-wall locations in small towns. One of the most fun stores is a family hardware store in a farming community. Use your imagination!

○ Set a date when you and your husband can take an entire day away.

○ Schedule a baby-sitter, if needed.

○ Clean up the car, and fill it with gas before you leave. Have enough money for the day (that is, so you can get back home!).

○ Take along your map.

○ Bring a camera to record the day's events.

○ Select the Let's Talk questions you would like to discuss with your husband (write them down or mark them in this book). Then take along either your list or this book so that you will remember what you want to talk about.

Choose an Unforgettable Tip and a Post-Date Idea from the lists below.

∼ ∼ ∼

### *Unforgettable Tips*

1. If your husband is a book lover, purchase a devotional book for him. Stuart Briscoe's *One Year Book of Devotions for Men* (Tyndale House) includes a CD format that can be used on an office computer. On the date, give your husband the book with a personal note from you on the inside cover.

2. Does your husband have a small or thinline Bible that he can carry in his briefcase or car? If not, purchase one for him. As an added bonus, have his name imprinted on the cover. (Many Christian bookstores offer this service for their Bibles.) Present this special Bible to him sometime during your date.

3. Give him a gift—a piece of rope (no, that's not a misprint). Buy a piece of rope that has three braided strands, or buy some rope and braid three pieces yourself. During the date, give it to your husband and tell him that it's a picture of your marriage—that you, he, and God are intimately connected. Tell him to keep that rope in his car, truck, or office as a constant reminder. Or here's another idea. Our friend Joe White uses a brass link as a reminder that he is forever linked to his wife. I keep a link on my key chain to remind myself of my link to Barb and Christ.

4. If he's a plant lover, purchase an indoor vine for his office. Remind him that Jesus is the vine, and he and you are the branches. Without Christ, you can do nothing (see John 15:5).

5. Get a copy of the *One Year Bible* (Tyndale House) and

share it with your husband. Each of you can read the day's readings separately, taking time to underline key thoughts and promises and to write comments in the margins. Barb and I do this daily, and we look forward to what the other is learning. Keep the Bible on a coffee table, the kitchen table, or somewhere you both will see it often in order to prompt you to have your personal time in the Word.

### Post-Date Ideas

1. Ask your husband every day, "What can I pray about for you today?" and then be sure to do it. Follow up. If he asks you to pray about a big meeting with a client, ask him later in the day how the meeting went.

2. Pray for your husband every day for the next thirty days. Whatever needs you sense he has (especially if he is not fulfilling the leadership role), pray that God will work in his life.

3. If, while studying the Bible, you read something that causes a question, bring it up with your husband. Ask for his insights. Share yours.

4. Begin to act on at least one comment that he made during the date.

5. Purchase a calendar. This could be any kind that works for you. Tell your husband that it will be in a location where both of you will see it every day, such as on the bedroom dresser. A pen will always be beside the calendar. On it, you both can write your prayer needs for that day—or upcoming days. It will be a way to be specific in your prayers for each other. You could purchase this calendar together as part of your date.

### Let's Talk

Choose some questions/comments from each level to help guide your discussion during your date. This way you can learn more about how you can meet your husband's need for spiritual intimacy and connection.

**LEVEL 1:**

*Dip Your Toes into the Water*

- "Tell me about your family's spiritual life as you were growing up. Did you go to church regularly? Did you pray as a family? What do you remember most?"
- "Tell me about your funniest camp or youth-group experience from your past."
- "In what areas did you often take on leadership as you were growing up? Does leadership come easily for you? Why or why not?"
- "Describe some of your family's Christmas and Easter traditions from when you were growing up. Which ones would you like to continue?"
- "Did your parents pray for you? What did that mean to you?"

**LEVEL 2:**

*Up to Your Ankles*

- You've probably heard about your husband's spiritual journey before, but ask him to tell you about it again.
- "What helps you grow closer to Christ? What things interfere with your spiritual life?"
- "What do you think your spiritual gifts are? How can you work at developing them, and how can I help you in this?"
- "What are the characteristics of a healthy church home? In what ways does our current church fit the bill? In what ways does it fall short?"
- "If you could meet anyone in the Bible, who would it be? Why? What would you ask him or her? What would you like to share with that person?"

**LEVEL 3:**

*Treading in Deeper Waters*

- "What do you think it means to be 'called' by God to do a

certain task or fill a particular function? Have you ever
been convinced that you were called to a ministry or job?
How?"

- "Do you trust God without reservations? If you have some,
what are they?"
- "At what times do you feel overwhelmed? How do your
body, emotions, and spirit react when that feeling hits?
What can I do to help?"
- "Do you have a regular time to pray and study the Bible? If
not, why not? If so, when do you do it? What are you reading?"
- "How often do you pray? What do you pray about?"

**LEVEL 4:**
### Bouncing on the Waves

- "Do you ever have doubts about God's character, about the
Bible, or about Jesus? How do you express these doubts?
How do they affect you?"
- "Are you satisfied with the time we spend together reading
the Bible and praying? What can we do together to meet
each other's needs in this area?"
- "How would you define your role as spiritual servant leader
of our household?"
- "How would you feel if all God asked you to do in life was
bring up your children to love and obey Jesus Christ—if
you never became rich or famous, but were 'ordinary'? If
you worked hard and served others when you could but
didn't leave a legacy that hundreds would praise you for,
would you feel as if you had a life worth living?"

**LEVEL 5:**
### Diving in Head First

- "In our prayer life together, how do we generally pray? Are
we praying for an easy life, or are we seeking to have God
strengthen us and deepen our character? How can we
improve our prayer life so that God is pleased?"

- "In what ways can I challenge you spiritually to excel—without nagging or making you feel inadequate?"
- "Do you feel that I am taking over in areas of leadership where I should not be? Where am I stepping on your toes? What can I do to step back and let you lead?"
- We shouldn't put our lives into compartments, but for a moment, examine these areas in your life together: *(a)* spiritual, *(b)* emotional, *(c)* physical, and *(d)* mental. Are you both supporting each other, growing in these areas, and feeling challenged? Then talk about why.

# Chapter Nine

# A Date to Meet My Husband's Need for Encouragement and Affirmation

Greg called into our daily national radio program recently and summed up what a lot of men experience. "I have a good life and family; I just thought it would be a little different from the way it has turned out, Gary and Barb. My work isn't going too well, finances are tight, I seem to be missing some signals from the kids, and I'm not feeling quite as trim and fit as I was a year ago." Barb and I gave him some coaching, and one of the recommendations was to talk with his wife about some of these stage-related experiences he was having and ask her to help him through them.

Two weeks later Greg called back in again with this update. "Before I called you a few weeks ago, I had never called a radio program in my life, and here I am calling a second time. But I just have to tell you what Shawna did. I followed your advice and shared some of the stuff I was going through. I came away from the time with Shawna feeling like a million bucks. She listened, affirmed me, and pointed out where I was winning as well as needing to improve. The bottom line is that she validated that what I was going through was pretty normal. Shawna shared with me that she has been praying for me and was waiting for me to bring up some of the things she was also concerned about. We prayed afterward, and then she snuggled up next to me and told me she was proud of me. I think what helped the most was that she let me know I didn't have to go through this stuff alone, that she and God were there to listen and to walk through it with me. Thanks for your help, but I think next time I'll just call Shawna instead of you guys."

Barb and I loved that call. And we loved hearing the story of a wife who encouraged her husband when he needed it. Way to go, Shawna!

### The Number Four Love Need of Men

How many of you were cheerleaders back in your high school days? I can picture some of you wildly jumping up and down and clapping your hands (no wonder you were cheerleaders!). Others of you are recalling those high school days and wouldn't have wanted to be a cheerleader if someone had paid you to do it.

Aside from all the popularity stuff that clung to the whole persona of the "cheerleader," consider what these girls (and guys) did. Their job was to "cheer on" the team on the field— to encourage them to do their best and then to scream and jump around wildly when they did.

Well, women, you don't have to be able to do the splits or clap and stomp at the same time, but you do need to be a cheer-leader every day for the "one-man team" in your life. Just as cheerleaders encourage the team when the game is going badly as well as when it is going well, so you need to be encouraging your husband on the bad days as well as the good days. He needs you to be there, always on his side, an ever loyal fan. He needs to know that he is special and that you are rooting for him.

If you look up the word *encouragement,* you'll find defini-tions and synonyms such as to cheer, comfort, hearten, inspire, buoy up, boost, invigorate, and do the heart good. What would your marriage be like if you consistently did this for your husband?

Incidentally, both husband and wives rated "encouragement" as their number four love need. Obviously, you want encouragement from us as much as we want encouragement from you. As different as we are from you women, in some ways we are alike. We're not impervious to the changes that age is causing in our lives. We don't like the extra weight or the changing (or disappearing) hairline any more than you like your extra weight or the wrinkles that are appearing out of nowhere. We notice that we can't do some of the things we used to be able to do. Whether we were sports fanatics in our younger years or not, if we haven't stayed in shape, we know it. We do silly things at times to prove that we've still "got it," only to end up sorry that we "tried it." Getting older is difficult. We need to know that you still see us as that "one-man team" that can be cheered on to victory!

Believe me, your voice cheering us on is the only human one we need (and truly long) to hear. As we shared in the last chapter, God's voice is essential as well.

## Your Husband's Cheering Section

I have discovered that men need the four *A*'s when it comes to encouragement: acceptance, access, attention, and affirmation.

- When you *accept* your husband, you're saying, "I would marry you all over again. You're not getting older, you're getting better."
- When you give your husband *access,* you give him a listening ear. He knows that he can talk to you about anything.
- When you give your husband *attention,* you not only give a listening ear, but you drop all other distractions that are vying for your attention and focus on him.
- When you *affirm* your husband, you remind him that you believe in him, you love him, and you'll stand by his side no matter what stresses threaten to overwhelm him. You let him know you'll get through it together.

When we receive this kind of encouragement from our wives, we are infused with new strength even if the day at work has been rotten. When we have this kind of encouragement, we become new men, ready to take on the world. This refreshment touches our souls. The world may beat us down, the boss may not appreciate us, the stress levels may be high, but we know that you are right there beside us, cheering us on. You know who we really are and what we are capable of doing; you trust us; you're ready to fight for us; and you're praying for us.

Perhaps that last one is the most important key. When we know that you are storming heaven on our behalf, we feel as if the armies of heaven itself are standing beside us. Your prayers mean the world to us, so don't stop praying. Pray for specifics. For example, pray that we will be faithful to God and that we will be hungry for God's Word. Pray that we'll be faithful to God on the job. Pray that we'll sense God's leading if it becomes apparent that we need to change careers. Pray for us through the stresses of our everyday routine. Pray that we'll be the kind of father we should be to our kids. Pray us through the choices and decisions we must make.

We're not going to become perfect. We have our flaws, our failures, and our weaknesses. As you pray, don't look for perfection. Instead, pray for God to work and then continue to encourage us every day of our lives. God is working in us and will change us in his time and in his way. In the meantime, your encouragement will go a long way toward helping us to become the men we want to be—for God and for you.

## Learn the Cheers

So what cheers does your husband need to hear? Your husband needs to be encouraged to hear the applause—that is, to know God's approval and your approval. Perhaps you are behind him, but how does he know if he can't hear you? If the cheerleaders are silent, the team will doubt their support. Your husband needs to *hear* your applause. Remind him of God's constant presence in his life. Tell him that he can go to God—and to you—anytime about anything. Be a loud voice of encouragement—a cheerleader he can hear!

Encourage your husband by reminding him of God's work in his life. Affirm what God is doing; tell him that you see God at work; affirm his spiritual gifts.

Encourage your husband to be accountable to other Christian men—and encourage him to build those kinds of friendships. Encourage him to connect with his children whenever you can. If you sense that there is distance between the kids and their dad, facilitate a time of togetherness. Send your daughter on a date with her dad; encourage him to take the boys for a guys' night out.

Finally, encourage him to reach out and grow—to take advantage of opportunities that will develop him as a man and deepen his spiritual life.

## Pre-Date Ideas

Before you consider the suggested dates in this section, I'd like you to think about your husband for a few minutes. Focus on the following questions:

_ How am I doing on the four A's with my husband? Do I accept him? Do I give him access, attention, and affirmation? If not, what can I do better? If so, does he know it?

_ Is my husband struggling with a disappointment, a failure, or a large amount of stress? In what ways am I being his cheerleader?

_ Do I encourage him in front of the children? What cues do the children take from me about their dad? What do I need to improve?

_ In what ways do I express the voice of God to my husband? In what ways am I not being that comforting, encouraging voice? How can I do better?

_ Are my words to my husband full of praise and encouragement, or are they more often critical and impatient?

We guys are working very hard for you. We love you. We
love our children. We may even love our jobs. If we don't, we
still go to work every day. We feel very keenly the responsibility
to provide for you a certain standard of living, a few things we
would like, college for the children, and a secure future.
Whether money comes easily or hard, we desire to always do
more and be more. We are competitive creatures by nature, and
our heaviest competitor may be ourselves. It's tough out there,
and we need to know that you are always there to support us.
We need to know that you love and appreciate us. We need to
know that you are the president of our fan club. And even if
you're the only member, you're the only member we need.

*Four Suggested Dates with Your Husband*

**DATE IDEA #1**

# Take Your Wife to Work Day
*(Rating: fairly flexible but must be planned ahead, easy to
prepare, low expense)*

What does your husband do every day at work? Do you really
know? One of the best ways to cheer him on is to know his
"game." After all, cheerleaders need to understand the game in
order to know which cheer to say when. No one does the
basketball cheers during a football game!

If possible, join your husband for a morning on the job.
You'll have to plan this ahead of time with him. Ask him for a
morning when you can just be with him. You can watch him
at work, learn about the job, or even help him. If your
husband's job doesn't allow for this during a workday, then
plan a Saturday morning when he can show you his workplace
and explain what he does and how he does it.

Your goal is to be able to visualize when he talks to you about his workday. You'll be able to picture what he's talking about. You can ask better questions; you can be more attuned to him. You can cheer him on even better!

Take your husband out for lunch, and discuss the Let's Talk questions.

### Prep Steps

○ Describe this date to your husband. Ask him to look at his schedule and decide on a time when you and he can do this date together. Get the date on the family calendar.

○ Schedule a baby-sitter, if needed.

○ If you work outside the home, arrange for a vacation day so you can enter your husband's world.

○ Dress appropriately for the date—depending on your husband's type of work. Dress in business clothes if he's at an office, your jeans and boots if he's on a construction site. Don't be late!

○ Plan for a lunch out with your husband. Ask him to take you to his favorite place. Or ask him to take you to the place he often goes for lunch during his workday (which may be the office cafeteria).

○ Select the Let's Talk questions you would like to discuss with your husband (write them down or mark them in this book). Then take along either your list or this book so that you will remember what you want to talk about.

Choose an Unforgettable Tip and a Post-Date Idea from the lists at the end of the chapter.

**DATE IDEA #2**

## A "Steak" Out

*(Rating: flexible, fairly easy to plan, medium expense)*

If your husband is like many men, a favorite meal is a big, juicy steak with all the trimmings. And if your household is like most households, steak is a luxury not consumed very often at home.

So, take your husband on a "steak" out. In other words, make reservations at the best steak house around (or maybe your husband would prefer to eat at a restaurant known for its ribs or seafood or Italian food). The point is, you're going to splurge on him for this special night out and treat him to the best meal ever. You want to encourage him by saying, "I want to lavish you with something that you'll completely enjoy—something that we don't do very often!"

During your dinner, discuss your questions from the Let's Talk section.

### Prep Steps

○ Decide the type of meal that will please your husband, or ask him where he would most like to go.

○ Make reservations, and put the date on your calendars. If possible, you might want to try to do this date on a week-night when the restaurant may be a bit quieter and there will be less chance of running into someone you know. When you make the reservations, ask for a quiet table.

○ Schedule a baby-sitter, if needed.

○ Dress appropriately for the location. (You might want to dress in an outfit that you know he loves to see you in.)

○ Turn on your answering machine before you leave, and turn off the cell phones. Minimizing distractions will be essential on this one. When your husband thinks he is getting all your attention, he wants *all* of it.

○ Select the Let's Talk questions you would like to discuss with your husband (write them down or mark them in this book). Then take along either your list or this book so that you will remember what you want to talk about.

Choose an Unforgettable Tip and a Post-Date Idea from the lists at the end of the chapter.

**DATE IDEA #3**

# Celebrate Your Husband

*(Rating: not flexible, will take a little planning, medium to high expense)*

You love your husband, and perhaps he has some special friends who love him too. This is a way to encourage your husband beyond what he could ever imagine. Invite a couple of his closest friends (and their wives, if they're married) to join you for an evening to celebrate your husband. You can plan to serve just dessert at your home, to go out for dessert (your treat), or to have a full-fledged dinner either at home or at a restaurant. If you go out to eat, you'll need to go to a place that will be conducive to the kind of sharing you want to have happen.

Tell those special friends to come prepared to "toast" your husband. Explain that this is meant to be a time of encouragement for your husband, so they should come prepared to tell him what a difference he has made in their lives, what they love about him, or what they appreciate about him.

Set aside some time afterward for the two of you to discuss the Let's Talk questions.

**Prep Steps**

○ Talk to your husband's close friends, and find a date that will work for everyone. Get the date on everyone's schedules. Make sure everyone knows that this is adults only and that each person is to come prepared to encourage your husband.

○ Have your husband put the date on his calendar. You could surprise him, or you could let him expect a dinner out with friends but not know the motivation behind it.

○ Plan the meal or dessert. If you're going to be at home, make this a special "dining room" meal with your best china and glassware. If you're going out, choose an appropriate location and make reservations.

○ You'll need to be the facilitator during the meal. After everyone has talked for a while, ask the friends to share their thoughts to encourage your husband.

○ Select the Let's Talk questions you would like to discuss with your husband (write them down or mark them in this book). Then take along either your list or this book so that you will remember what you want to talk about.

Choose an Unforgettable Tip and a Post-Date Idea from the lists at the end of the chapter.

**DATE IDEA #4**
# All in the Family
*(Rating: flexible, easy to plan, low to medium expense)*

One of the key issues involved in encouraging your husband is to continue to connect him with his children—and grandchildren if you are in that stage of life. Perhaps you feel as if your relationship with him is fine, but he's just not connecting with the kids because of time or other issues.

So your job is to plan a family date where you all can have a good time together. This can be simple—like spending the afternoon flying a kite or playing croquet. You could take the family to a fun movie, or rent a movie to watch at home. If you have family home videos, pull out a few of those and watch those little babies grow into adults (and watch the adults lose hair and gain weight!). That will be good for a few laughs! Maybe grab a board game all can enjoy.

Pop some popcorn, order pizza, or go out to eat at a fun place. Do whatever would make for a fun and memorable evening for your kids, you, and especially your husband.

Set aside some time later when the two of you are alone to discuss the Let's Talk questions.

## Prep Steps

○ Clear the decks for a family day (or evening). If you've

got older children, this may be a bit harder. Make sure
everyone has this time on their schedules and that nothing will be allowed to interfere.

○ Decide what you're going to do—ask your family, or
make it a surprise.

○ Make the necessary arrangements (renting a movie, finding out the movie times, making reservations, whatever).

○ If appropriate, take along a camera or video camera and
record the event for future memories.

○ Select the Let's Talk questions you would like to discuss
with your husband (write them down or mark them in
this book). Then take along either your list or this book
so that you will remember what you want to talk about.

Choose an Unforgettable Tip and a Post-Date Idea from the
lists below.

~~~

### *Unforgettable Tips*

1. Tell him, "I would marry you all over again. You're not
getting older—you're getting better! Okay, you are
getting older but I love you more every day."

2. If you're a frustrated poet, write a little cheer for your
husband. Read it to him (or cheer it for him—complete
with a couple jumps!). Laugh about it, but this little
cheer might become a part of your own private language
when your husband needs encouragement in the future.

3. Frame a picture of yourself. Find a way to include on the
picture or on the frame the words, "Your Number One
Fan!" (Or get a picture of the whole family, and have it
say, "Dad's Fans!") Give the picture to your husband on
the date.

4. If your husband is struggling with discouragement in
other areas of his life, take both of his hands in yours,
look him in the eyes, and say, "I believe in you. I'm with

you—sticking to you like superglue. Nothing's going to break us apart. We'll get through this together."

## Post-Date Ideas

1. When your husband needs to talk to you about some discouragement, set everything aside and listen.
2. Encourage your husband to stay connected to his children. Help him to plan a date with each of the kids individually. Consider making it a regularly scheduled time with his children. Moms are natural connectors of dads and kids. Barb has modeled this for our family.
3. Talk to him about being involved with other Christian men in a Bible study or accountability group. Tell him that if he wants to do that, you'll clear the decks for him to be able to have that time. Make some muffins, chili, or some of his favorite treats, and encourage him to welcome his buddies to your home.
4. Begin to work on at least one thing that you both talked about in your discussion time.

## Let's Talk

Choose some questions/comments from each level to help guide your discussion during your date. This way you can learn more about how you can meet your husband's need for encouragement and affirmation.

### LEVEL 1:

### Dip Your Toes into the Water

- "In what areas does my encouragement mean the most to you?"
- "What is the best compliment I could give you?"
- "Do I thank you enough for all that you do for me (and the kids), or do you feel taken for granted? How can I improve? What would help you to feel appreciated?"

- "Do I say 'I love you' too much, too little, or often enough?"
- "Do you think you are competitive in sports, games, at work, or at home? What drives your competition? Is it ever unhealthy? Why or why not?"

## LEVEL 2:
### Up to Your Ankles

- "Do I praise you enough in front of others? What kind of praise would you like? What kind of praise would make you uncomfortable?"
- "What's the difference between encouraging you and complimenting you?"
- "Do you think that you spend most of your time doing what you are well suited to do? If not, what needs to change? What would you most enjoy doing on a daily basis?"
- "What do you think your spiritual gifts are? How can you work at developing them, and how can I help you in this?"
- "Does it ever seem that I'm not giving you my full attention when you're talking to me? When does that happen? What needs to change?"

## LEVEL 3:
### Treading in Deeper Waters

- "How am I helping or hindering you in reaching your potential? In what specific ways could I help?"
- "Do you feel that I cheer you on, or am I usually either silent or negative? How would you like me to cheer you on? In what areas do you especially need it?"
- Tell your husband how often you think of him during the day. Explain how those thoughts of him make you feel.
- "When do you judge yourself the most harshly? How should I respond when that happens? Do I ever judge you harshly? If so, in what situations?"
- Complete this sentence for your husband: "As we grow older together, I love you more because . . ."

**LEVEL 4:**

*Bouncing on the Waves*

- "When you try something and fail, how should I respond? What will be the most helpful to you?"
- "In what five ways can I inspire you to do and be your best?"
- "Are you ever envious of what others have or what others are doing with their lives? If so, what makes you feel that way? How do you respond to those feelings?"
- "Who are your closest male friends? Do you feel as if they are challenging you, holding you accountable, or helping you to grow spiritually? What needs to change?"

**LEVEL 5:**

*Diving in Head First*

- Tell your husband in what ways and in what areas you see him reaching his fullest potential. Describe how his life is giving back to you, to your children, and to God.
- List five positive things you see in your husband in each of the following areas: achievements, service to God and others, special talents and skills, character qualities, childrearing.
- "Is there anything about life in general or our current circumstances that discourages or disappoints you? What can I do to help turn that around?"
- "Booker T. Washington said, 'Success is measured not so much by the position that one has reached in life as by the obstacles which he has overcome while trying to succeed.' Is this a true statement in your opinion? What obstacles have we overcome as a couple? In what ways are we truly successful?"
- Tell your husband five things that you find worthy of respect and admiration in his life.

# ~Chapter Ten~

# A Date to Meet My Husband's Need for Friendship

Brandon's wife, Jennifer, loved to hang out with her older three sisters. When Karen, Amy, or Mandy walked in the door, Brandon knew it was going to be a slumber party full of words, laughter, emotion, tears, and . . . well, "chemistry." Jennifer knew how to connect; she was all female. And Brandon was all male. He thoroughly enjoyed competition, a hard run, and heading to the woods for a weekend hunting trip.

Recently Brandon was really needing to connect to Jennifer, yet she was struggling trying to meet his deep companionship needs. When all the sisters were together one night, they started talking about their husband's friendship needs. Jennifer was full of questions, and her older sisters stepped in to give her some sisterly coaching.

"My husband needs me to play with him, Jennifer," said Karen. "When I watch a game with him or pick him up a fishing magazine, he beams."

"I've been trying to remind my husband that his feelings are valid and real," Amy shared. "He didn't grow up in a family where feelings were safe, and I'm trying to let him know that when he is frustrated, anxious, or feeling rejected, it is okay to feel those emotions. They are natural, and they come and go. It doesn't mean there is anything wrong."

Mandy had a different slant on helping her little sister connect to Brandon. "The biggest thing I've found is that my husband doesn't want to be misunderstood. He really feels judged when I tell him what he is feeling rather than ask him."

Jennifer was all ears, and later that weekend she talked with Brandon about his friendship needs. She confessed that she couldn't meet them all, but she wanted to continue to love him the way he needed to be loved: in all his God-given masculinity, not trying to make him one of her sisters but connecting to his love needs by entering his world and becoming his *best* friend.

Jennifer didn't grow up with brothers, so it didn't come naturally to her to tune into Brandon's companionship needs, but she was teachable. If you need some help understanding your husband's needs, maybe some of the following discussion will help you get a handle on how he's wired and how you can begin to meet his need for friendship.

## The Number Three Love Need of Men

Who are your husband's friends? Who is his best friend? Why are these people so important to him?

Did you know, however, that your husband has a desire for a special best friend, someone who is already a regular part of his life? Did you know that this "somebody" is *you?* Believe it or not, your husband wants you to be his best friend. Not his best "bud," but his best friend.

We discovered in our survey that the top three love needs of men correspond with three different types of love described in the Bible with three different Greek words. *Agape,* unconditional love, is a man's top love need. *Eros,* romantic, sexual love, is his number two love need. *Phileo,* friendship love, is his number three love need. Clearly, we men need a lot of loving!

The friendship we have with you is very different from what we have with our guy friends. Sure, we like our buddies, those guys we hang out with or do certain activities with. But, as you already know all too well, we're *guys*. So along with the territory of our friendships comes lots of friendly competition (we just can't seem to help it) and not much vulnerability (we can't help that either). We have this sort of "macho" switch that kicks in with our buddies. We don't want to admit that we've got a problem, that we can't handle something, or that we need help. If we feel inadequate, then we think we look like jerks to our friends.

You see, with your female friends, it's very different. You can cry together, worry together, and talk through problems together. You'll talk a lot, share a whole range of emotions, and no one feels threatened or stupid. In fact, such vulnerability only increases your affection for one another. You feel as if you've been let into each other's worlds, and you really care and nurture one another.

You're not going to get that with your husband—and he doesn't necessarily want that kind of constant intensity from you. But he does want—and need—you to be his very best friend.

## Soul Mates

Being your husband's best friend is a relationship that reaches way down into both of your souls. Your husband needs to know that there is one person in his life whom he can count on, no matter what. Best friends receive each other through the good times and the bad. They're always there in the routine of life. They go through everything together. They are "soul mates."

This friendship love bonds you together. In the sharing of experiences, of feelings, and of hearts your souls bond. Friendship love sustains the relationship as it sails along on most of its pretty routine days. It is comfortable—like an old pair of jeans and a ragged sweatshirt.

Your husband wants to be comfortable with you. He also knows, deep down, that he wants to be safe with you, to explore what is going on in his mind and heart—the kind of vulnerability that he most likely won't get anywhere else (from his golfing buddies, for example). He wants to be able to take risks with you, knowing that he won't be judged or rejected. He wants to reach out, but he doesn't want to be misunderstood.

I hope that you and your husband had a chance to be friends before you were married. That friendship should carry over and continue. Many couples, however, get into the romance so quickly that they don't develop the friendship. When they get married and the spark of romance fizzles with the arrival of children or financial hardships, they don't have the friendship to carry them through.

Friendship in marriage is vital. So how do you, as a woman, become your husband's best friend?

## He Needs You to Be There

To develop your friendship with your husband, you need to have realistic expectations of what that friendship looks like. As I noted above, your husband is not going to be "one of the girls." He's not going to express deep emotions regularly. He's not going to reach deep down and be vulnerable quite so easily.

Tell your husband you want to be his best friend. Be there for him. When he does open up and is vulnerable with you, listen to what he says. Don't judge. Rather, validate his feelings, encourage him, and remind him that you will never leave. If you need to speak the truth to him, do so lovingly. And always keep whatever he says completely confidential.

We are men in process. We are learning and growing and changing. We can be receptive and teachable when you come to us with the truth couched in words of comfort and encouragement. We appreciate it when you wait for the right time, when you wait for us to be vulnerable.

We desire forgiveness. We want to be able to take the past and leave it there—in the past. We need to work through problems with you and then, when we have done so, trust that forgiveness is complete.

And we want you to enter our world. Sure, we have our buddies, but once in a while, we'd love you to come fishing, or golfing, or bowling along with us. We don't care if you're not good at it; we just want to share the experience with you. We don't care if the activity is not your passion; we just care that *we* are your passion! When you come along with us, when you step into our world, you're saying, "I'm passionate about *you!*"

And that kind of passion can last a lifetime!

## Pre-Date Ideas

Before you consider the suggested dates in this section, I'd like you to think about your husband for a few minutes. Focus on the following questions:

- _ Do I think of my husband as my best friend? Have I been a best friend to him? In what ways?
- _ Does my husband feel free to be open and vulnerable with me? Why or why not?
- _ Does my husband feel safe with me? Are we comfortable together?
- _ In what ways have I been forgiving or unforgiving toward him over hurts and disappointments in the past?
- _ When was the last time I entered his world and was his companion in something important to him?

Life will change—that's a given. In your marriage you will experience many changes. Life may throw some curveballs that you aren't expecting. Difficulties may arise. As you age, other things occur as your own parents age or die. Your children grow and leave home. Your career changes and eventually ends. The only constant through all of this is each other. You will be with your husband through it all. That's where your friendship love kicks in. It carries you along, for you are soul mates, and you realize that you simply need the other person to complete you.

Your husband needs you. He wants you to be there through it all. He wants to know that you will stick to him like glue for the rest of your lives.

*Four Suggested Dates with Your Husband*

**DATE IDEA #1**

# His Favorite Movie

*(Rating: very flexible, easy to plan, low expense)*

Plan a special evening at home with your husband. This is a way to have a night "out" even if you can't get out because of limited money or tight schedules or children's needs.

Find out the name of your husband's all-time favorite movie. On the night of your date, get the video from the video store or the local library. Your goal for this evening is to step into your husband's world, to learn more about him, to find out what makes him tick. Watch the movie, and try to see it through his eyes.

Don't forget about serving up some of his favorite goodies while you watch the movie. Afterward, talk about why this is his favorite movie. This can lead into a time of talking about the Let's Talk questions.

### Prep Steps

○ You don't have to plan ahead for this one. Be spontaneous. Just make sure your husband knows ahead of time by saying something like, "Tomorrow night we're going to have a special night together."

○ Ask him what his all-time favorite movie is.

○ Go to the video store or library, and check out the tape.

○ Purchase snacks to eat during the movie.

○ Select the Let's Talk questions you would like to discuss with your husband (write them down or mark them in this book). Then take along either your list or this book so that you will remember what you want to talk about.

Choose an Unforgettable Tip and a Post-Date Idea from the lists at the end of the chapter.

**DATE IDEA #2**

# Be His Favorite Student

*(Rating: flexible, may not take much planning, varies in expense depending on the activity)*

I've mentioned the importance of being a student of your husband. Think about him for a moment. Does he have a hobby that he is passionate about? What does he do in his spare time? Is he constantly in the garden or fiddling with the engine of that old car? Is he a real student of the Civil War, or is he always reading about antique cars?

Whatever his interest or passion, your job is to figure out a way to jump in and be involved with him. Work with him for an afternoon in the garage. Watch him work on that engine; have him explain it to you; ask him to teach you some basics. Learn the names of the tools he needs.

If he's a Civil War buff, tell him you want to spend an afternoon learning about it. Go to a museum together, rent a movie about the Civil War, or look through some of those big picture books that you can get from the library (or that he already owns!). Have him teach you. Discover why it interests him so much. If his interest is antique cars, get tickets to a car show or a museum. Have him teach you all that he can about the cars. Discover why this is a passion for him.

After sharing in one of these activities, spend some time talking about the Let's Talk questions.

### Prep Steps

○ Talk to your husband about his favorite things to do. If he has an obvious hobby, tell him you want to join him in that hobby for a day. Focus on your husband, learn all that you can about his hobby and about him as you watch him at work. No fair getting distracted or bored too easily. Do what you can to learn and to help.

○ If you need to purchase tickets to a show or museum, do so. Do whatever preparations may be required.

○ Get the date for joining your husband's hobby on everyone's calendar. Even if you're just going to be at home, set aside the time so that nothing else gets in the way.

○ Schedule a baby-sitter, if needed.

○ Select the Let's Talk questions you would like to discuss with your husband (write them down or mark them in this book). Then take along either your list or this book so that you will remember what you want to talk about.

Choose an Unforgettable Tip and a Post-Date Idea from the lists at the end of the chapter.

**DATE IDEA #3**

## A Play Date

*(Rating: flexible, may take some creative thinking as some of these depend on seasons, locations, etc., low to medium expense)*

You've heard of moms who set up "play dates" for their kids to play with other kids. Well, you're going to plan a "play date" for you and your husband.

When was the last time you laughed and just had fun together? For too many couples it has been too long. This date also has several different variations—but the key point is playing together. So let me give you some options: Go to the fair, and ride the silly bumper rides. Go sledding down your favorite hill. Play in the waves at the beach. Go to the local playground, and push each other on the swings. Get a Frisbee, and throw it at the park. Fly a kite. Shoot some hoops. Go rollerblading.

Get it? Go and have fun by playing together. Laugh a lot. Go out for ice cream (or hot chocolate) afterward for your quiet time together to talk.

### Prep Steps

○ Get the date on everyone's calendar.

○ Schedule a baby-sitter, if needed.

○ Decide on what type of date you'll be doing, and give your husband a heads up.

○ Get together whatever you may need for the date—sleds, a kite, the Frisbee hidden away in the garage, the rollerblades from the back of the closet.

○ Have fun!

○ Select the Let's Talk questions you would like to discuss with your husband (write them down or mark them in this book). Then take along either your list or this book so that you will remember what you want to talk about.

Choose an Unforgettable Tip and a Post-Date Idea from the lists at the end of the chapter.

**DATE IDEA #4**

## Sports Fans

*(Rating: not flexible, must be planned ahead, may be expensive)*

Is your husband an avid sports fan? Which sport and which team are his favorites? If you are a sports fan too, this one won't be too hard. But if you aren't, then you will need to do a little research. (If you don't know your husband's favorite teams, for instance, a look at his caps in the closet may tell you.) Arrange tickets to a game. If the team is local, you're in luck. If not, then you'll have to research and find out if/when that team is playing a local team and get tickets for that game. Be sure to get really good seats—even if they cost extra. If you don't know where the good seats are, find someone who does know and can advise you.

Perhaps your husband already has season tickets. Then accompany him to the game. Tell him you want to spend the evening with him—enjoying the game and also having a meal afterward.

If you are not familiar with your husband's favorite sports but really want to score some points—no pun intended—read up about the team before the date. Find out the names of the starters. Learn some of the rules of the game so you can follow it and not ask too many questions.

Set aside a time afterward, perhaps over a dinner out, to discuss your Let's Talk questions.

Who knows? You may find yourself hooked!

## Prep Steps

○ Research when and where his favorite team will be play-ing. Research the best seating location. Purchase the tickets.

○ Get the date on everyone's calendar.

○ Schedule a baby-sitter, if needed.

○ Do some research about the sport and the team. Learn as much as you can ahead of time.

○ Select the Let's Talk questions you would like to discuss with your husband (write them down or mark them in this book). Then take along either your list or this book so that you will remember what you want to talk about.

Choose an Unforgettable Tip and a Post-Date Idea from the lists below.

~ ~ ~

## Unforgettable Tips

1. Purchase something that will be a reminder of your date: a new tool for his hobby; a new cap or jersey of his favorite team; a new baseball glove.
2. Remind your husband that your relationship is a secure and safe place to sort out whatever is going on in his heart. Anytime. Anyplace.
3. Tell him that you are doing this date because you long to enter his world as his friend. He is important to you. You want to know him on a deeper level.

## Post-Date Ideas

1. Find a way to keep the date going. For example, take whatever opportunities you can to play together. Or follow his favorite team's exploits each day in the paper. Or pay attention to whatever you find that might be of interest regarding his hobby.
2. Whenever your husband wants to talk to you, drop everything and give him your undivided attention.
3. It can be easy to let those little "irritations" continue to eat away at you, even as you go on these dates and seek to be your husband's friend. Work together to resolve anything that is getting in the way. Keep perspective on the "little" irritants—if they're "little," do they really deserve your full attention? Where can you let up and allow your husband some breathing room?
4. Put into practice at least one thing you and your husband talked about.

## Let's Talk

Choose some questions/comments from each level to help guide your discussion during your date. This way you can learn more about how you can meet your husband's need for friendship.

**LEVEL 1:**

### Dip Your Toes into the Water

- "What are a few things that refresh you the most?"
- "What's your favorite sport to play? Why do you like it? Do you feel that you're good at it? What is your favorite sport to watch? Why?"
- "What's your favorite hobby? When you have some free time, what do you like to do most?"
- "If you could write a book, what would you title it? What would it be about? How much would you sell it for?"
- "Who are your best friends? Why do they mean so much to you?"

**LEVEL 2:**

### Up to Your Ankles

- "Describe two of your favorite memories of things we've done together."
- "What do you enjoy most about your life? What would you like to change?"
- "What do you enjoy most about your job (career)? What would you like to change?"
- "If you had to (or wanted to) leave the career you're in, what other job or career do you see yourself entering?"
- "Are there times when you wish that I would join you, but you just haven't asked because you think I wouldn't want to? What activities would you like me to do with you?"

**LEVEL 3:**

### Treading in Deeper Waters

- "Describe three ways that we could enjoy each other more."
- "Do you ever feel lonely even though we're sitting in the same room together? What can I do to keep you from feeling that way?"

- "Do you ever fear the future? How can I best help you to deal with those fears?"
- "What are three goals you are working on right now in your life? How can I support you in these?"
- "Share three things about your growing up years that you have never told me."

**LEVEL 4:**
### Bouncing on the Waves

- "How would you describe our friendship before we got married? Is it any different now? How is my friendship with you different from your friendship with your guy friends?"
- "Why do friendships between men seem more superficial than those between women? Do you think that males in general have the capacity to be friends with very many people?"
- "Are you vulnerable with me, or do you hold a lot back that I should know about your life, your feelings, your thoughts? If you are not being vulnerable, why not?"
- "How can we set the right atmosphere in our marriage so that both of us feel safe sharing secrets and feelings with each other?"
- "In what ways do you look forward to growing old together? In what ways does that prospect not look so fun?"

**LEVEL 5:**
### Diving in Head First

- "Do you feel safe with me? Do you feel that you can be vulnerable with me and not face criticism or judgment? In what ways do I need to improve?"
- Tell your husband that you want to be his best friend. Ask him to list five things that you can do to be his best friend.
- "Do I ever bring up hurts or disappointments from the past? In what ways do I need to be more forgiving? How can I best do this for you?"

- "Do you think I am honest with you? If so, am I doing it in the right way at the right time? In what ways do you think I am dishonest? How can I correct that?"
- "Do you feel that I have any unrealistic expectations of you? In what ways and in what areas? What do you need me to do differently?"

# ~ Chapter Eleven ~

# A Date to Meet My Husband's Need for Sexual Intimacy

"Hi, Linda, may I speak to David?" asked Marcie as she called her husband at his office on Friday afternoon.

"Hi, honey. I know you have a busy day, but I cut out of work early and want to know if I can pick you up at the office at three o'clock?" Marcie asked in her most provocative voice.

"Yeah, I have a meeting in an hour, but I think I can break out of here at three. But what's up? Doesn't Jason have basketball after school? And wasn't Emma going to work at our house on her science project with her group?" David responded with a little more stress in his voice than either of them realized he was experiencing.

"I have it all taken care of. See you at three. And don't even think about being late," she responded with a knowing laugh.

What David didn't realize was that he was about to be kidnapped by his wife. He had been under a lot of pressure recently at his office, and the demands of the kids pressed in on them too. As a result, his physical relationship with Marcie had taken on a little too much of the "same old-same old."

Marcie decided to do something about it. After twenty-plus years of marriage she didn't want their sexual relationship to become predictable. And this plan was anything but predictable.

Marcie had arranged for a woman from her Bible study to stay with the kids for the next thirty-six hours. She went to her favorite intimate apparel store and picked out something that made her blush with the best of them. Then she stopped and bought a new silk robe for her husband along with his favorite chocolate-covered strawberries.

Then she went home and packed some lotions, scented candles, sparkling cider, and their favorite mood music on CD. She put on a dress David found attractive and the perfume he bought her three years ago for Christmas.

She and David had always talked about spending a night at the little bed-and-breakfast place their best friends had talked about over and over, so she had the place booked for a night. She even opted to pay extra and get a room with a hot tub.

When David came out of his office and took one look at his wife, he was a goner. It didn't take more than a nanosecond for him to get the drift—this was going to be an event he would remember!

In a phrase, Marcie had hit a grand slam and was rounding the bases to a standing ovation in David's favorite ballpark!

## The Number Two Love Need of Men

As I noted in the previous chapter, our survey showed that husbands have three different kinds of love as their top three love needs. Coming in at number two is *eros*—romantic love, sexual intimacy.

Some of you are saying sarcastically, "Well, *that's* a big surprise!" You wives need to understand, however, that your number two love need is very similar. Both husbands and wives desire intimacy—however, for you, *intimacy* is spelled T-A-L-K. For men, *intimacy* is spelled S-E-X. Both husbands and wives desire the closeness that comes from intimacy. The love need is the same, but the way it needs to be fulfilled is often quite differ-ent between men and women. You probably view intimacy as a

heart-to-heart talk in front of a roaring fire; your husband probably visualizes something else going on in front of that fire!

However, I cannot emphasize enough that your husband's
sex drive doesn't make him a dirty old man. Far from it. God
wired us men with a strong sex drive. We think about sex
often because sexual intimacy is a very real and vital need for
us. We men find our masculinity in our sexuality. Although
percentages differ from man to man, men report that from 50
to 90 percent of their self-image is locked up in their sexuality.
That's huge! Sex, passion, pleasing his wife sexually—it's a big
part of what makes a man feel like a man.

You see, your husband isn't at all weird! He's normal.
Husbands need sex with their wives, and they need it on a
regular basis (most men at least once or twice a week—
more for some). When you respond to your husband sexually, you affirm him beyond anything you could imagine.
A husband who is treated this way will often respond with
that emotional intimacy that his wife so desires—not as a
reward for sex, but as a natural outflow of a satisfying relationship.

On the other hand, when you rebuff his sexual advances,
when you're always too tired, or if you withhold sex because
you're out of sorts for other reasons, then you're emasculat-
ing your husband. You're hurting him where it hurts the
most. In response, he may stop meeting *your* need for
emotional intimacy—again not necessarily in a manipulative
way but just because your marriage will not be satisfying to
him and he will withdraw. Then begins a downward spiral
that has been a strong factor in the deterioration of many
marriages.

### He Needs You to Need Him

Sometimes we men can drive our wives crazy. (There's another
big surprise!) No matter how tired or stressed we may be,

we're just about always ready for sex. You see, we have an uncanny ability to compartmentalize our lives. Everything in our lives sits around in separate boxes. We have a work box, a church box, a friendship box, etc. When there's a problem in one box, it doesn't necessarily affect any of the other boxes. So we may be very stressed at work, but that doesn't affect our sex box! It's ready to be opened at a moment's notice!

Your wiring is different, however. Your boxes are all connected, so that if you are feeling stress in one box, all the rest are affected. So if you're having a lot of stress at work, that affects the family, the church activities, and, oh yes, sex. And if you are feeling stressed because of your husband—look out! Sex will be the last thing you want when you realize, for example, that he didn't do something you had requested or if he hurt you in some way.

But you see, we *need* you to need us. We have a need for sexual intimacy with you that is so strong that when met, we're on top of the world; when not met, we feel as if we are failures. Trust me on this. We need you to want us so much that once in a while *you* initiate sex; we get discouraged if you don't express passion for us. We struggle with feelings of inadequacy sexually because we so much want to please you. When we initiate sex with you, we want you to respond to us passionately. It hurts us terribly when you don't make time for us, when other activities are more important, or when you rebuff us continually.

When a husband's sexual needs aren't being met by his wife, he will feel rejected. When you refuse to meet his need (which is a legitimate, God-created need), you're telling him that his need is not important to you. If that continues, he will shut down or pull away from you. He'll quit trying for fear of further rejection. He'll pull away emotionally (which means that your love need for emotional intimacy will not be met). He'll spend more time at work or in other activities. Some men will be able to continue that unhappy pattern; however, others will find themselves looking elsewhere to have their needs met. While a man is ultimately responsible for his own moral decisions, his wife plays a key role in keeping him from desiring to meet his God-given sexual needs in any place other than his marriage.

You, his wife, are the one person chosen by God to meet your husband's sexual needs. You have the privilege—yes, *privilege*—of being the sole person to experience that deep level of intimacy with your husband.

## Meeting Your Husband's Sexual Love Need

For some women, this will be very easy. Perhaps your sex drive is just as strong as your husband's. Perhaps you just didn't realize how much your husband needs you, and you're ready and willing to meet his need. Go for it! You won't be sorry (and your husband will be thrilled!).

For some women, however, this will be very difficult. Some women are dealing with past emotional or sexual abuse that is affecting how they view sex now. Others were told by their parents that men want only one thing or that sex is always dirty. Such thinking completely distorts what should be a natural and joyful part of the marriage relationship. Think about it: God created sex. He could have created Adam and Eve to reproduce by means of spores sent through the air; instead, he created a physical act that allows for great intimacy and enjoyment. That's what sex with your husband is supposed to be.

Your sexual relationship often acts as a barometer for other problems in the marriage. It is a proven fact that a couple's sexual relationship is directly related to the experiences they bring into a marriage or to those that occur outside the marriage bed. But wounds can be healed. Whatever is going on, talk to God about it. If you and your husband are having problems sexually, ask God to help you understand what is going on deep inside you. If there is hurt, ask God to help you. If there is baggage, ask for his freedom. Start with your own heart. Unresolved pain causes many women great difficulty when it comes to opening up their hearts and their bodies to their husbands (remember the boxes?). If you need some extra help, find a good Christian counselor. I also recommend Dan Allender's book *The Wounded Heart* (NavPress), which helps men and women who have been abused or influenced by abuse walk through the pain. Also check out any medical issues with your physician.

How do you begin to meet your husband's need for sexual intimacy? One of the things that Barb and I stress when we lead our conferences is for husbands and wives to study each other. Do you know what signals he's giving when he wants to make love to you? Do you know—or care—what pleases him sexually? How frequently does he want (actually, it's *need*) sex? If you haven't been able to be intimate for a while, how does he react? Some men become short-tempered with everyone when they haven't been able to be intimate with their wives. In short, you need to know what your husband needs so then you can know how, and how often, to meet that need.

Remember, your husband's sexuality is so entwined with his masculinity that as you reach out to him and meet his need for sexual intimacy, you will affirm his God-given masculinity. So be passionate about your husband! Be passionate *with* your husband!

## Pre-Date Ideas

Before you consider the suggested dates in this section, I'd like you to think about your husband for a few minutes. Focus on the following questions:

- _ Do I understand that my husband's need for sex is normal? How often does he need sex? In what ways have I been fulfilling or not fulfilling this need for him?
- _ What satisfies or does not satisfy him about our sexual relationship? What would he want to change?
- _ Do I ever initiate sex? Why or why not? If I haven't been

doing it, how do I think he would respond if I did? What's holding me back?

_ What situations in my past are affecting my ability to respond sexually to my husband? What do I need to do to deal with these?

There's a reason why sex is your husband's number two love need. It's part of his wiring; it's the way he was created. You want to make your husband feel on top of the world? Express your passion for him; fulfill his sexual needs; and let him know that you want him just as much as he wants you.

Are things a little tense between you right now? Express your passion for him; fulfill his sexual needs; and let him know that you want him just as much as he wants you (even if it doesn't seem like it right now).

Get the picture? When you meet his need for sexual intimacy, you have shown him how important he and his needs are to you. He'll respond—I know! I've seen marriages that were on the brink end up being saved when the husband and wife reached out to each other and met their needs for intimacy—both the sexual intimacy most husbands need and the emotional intimacy most wives need. It's never too late to try.

Let me just say a few words to those of you who might be a little embarrassed as you read these suggested dates because they're about—well—sex! Remember a couple of things—this is your husband we're talking about. The man you've already had sex with a few times (we assume!), the man who fathered your children, if you have kids, and the man whom you know well and who knows you. When you plan this kind of a date for him, you're giving him an incredible gift. If you're embarrassed, all you need to do is provide the setting and the willingness—he'll take it from there! We've shared some of these ideas before in the FamilyLife product called "Simply Romantic Nights," to which Barb and I contributed. This is one of the hottest products we have seen in Christian publishing. It contains a sexual inventory for husbands and wives, a booklet about sexual intimacy, and twenty-four date ideas that will light your fire.

*Four Suggested Dates with Your Husband*

♡ **DATE IDEA #1**
## Let's Do Lunch
*(Rating: flexible, easy to prepare, low expense)*

Depending on your husband's line of work, he may "do lunch" with all kinds of people—boring people, interesting people, people he can help, people who can help him. Lunch often is merely an extension of his job, a time of doing business in a different setting.

Well, it's time for you to get down to business with him. By e-mail, phone call, or even fax machine, schedule a lunch date with your husband. It needs to be on his calendar as part of his schedule. On your note or in your call, tell him to meet you at home for lunch. (If this is a fax, don't embarrass him; be very professional. If not, then you can be as teasing as you want to be.)

Set up a lunch at home. You could use a picnic theme and have some lunch ready on a blanket (include some pillows in the scene) on the living room floor. Or perhaps you'll want to make a very light lunch to eat quickly.

Dress in something alluring. Greet him with a passionate kiss at the door. We'll leave the rest to you. Unless he can take the afternoon off, you might want to save your Let's Talk questions for a separate time—but schedule that as well.

If your husband's schedule doesn't allow for this kind of time off during the week, plan your lunch or dinner date on a weekend.

After your lunch date, call, fax, or write and tell your husband you'd like to have lunch again sometime—soon!

## Prep Steps

○ Send your husband the invitation, and put the date on your calendars.

○ If you have children, this is a great date to do while they are at school. If not, you might be able to have a neighbor watch your children during the lunch hour.

○ Prepare a light lunch.

○ Decide on any "setting" you want at home.

○ Find your sexiest dress or nightgown to wear. Splash on some of his favorite perfume.

○ Select the Let's Talk questions you would like to discuss with your husband (write them down or mark them in this book). Then take along either your list or this book so that you will remember what you want to talk about.

Choose an Unforgettable Tip and a Post-Date Idea from the lists at the end of the chapter.

**DATE IDEA #2**

# Mysterious Turn-On
*(Rating: flexible, easy to prepare, low expense)*

Is your husband one of those guys who loves detective movies or TV shows? Is he always reading mysteries? Then here's a date that will cause him to turn off the TV and turn on to you.

Plan an evening for your encounter with your husband. Be sure his agenda is clear and that he knows you're planning an evening at home.

For about four days before the night of your date, send him a ransom note each day. Make them look like ransom notes by cutting out letters from magazines to spell out the words. The first day, have a note that says, "Find me" or "Meet me—come alone." Use a pet name to sign it. The second day, have the note say, "Bring your body to [address] on [date]." The third day, give him the time to meet you. The fourth day, say, "Follow my directions—you'll know what I mean when you

get there." Each day, put the note in a location where he's sure
to find it—a lunch box, a coat or pants pocket, a day planner,
the seat of his car—be creative, but don't embarrass him!
These are for his eyes only.

The night of the date, leave a trail of your clothing from the
door he usually enters to wherever you'll be waiting for him.
Again, the rest is up to you.

Later in the evening, spend some time talking about your
Let's Talk questions.

### Prep Steps

○ Get the evening on your schedules. Your husband doesn't
   need to know about the content of the date, just that he
   should plan to keep the evening free.

○ If you have children, get a baby-sitter who will take them
   out of the house for the evening.

○ Prepare your ransom notes. Cut letters out of the newspaper or magazines. Think of places to put your notes
   each day.

○ Plan the setting—lighting, clothing, etc. If you have time
   beforehand, take a nice bath with lots of good-smelling
   bath oil!

○ Select the Let's Talk questions you would like to discuss
   with your husband (write them down or mark them in
   this book). Then take along either your list or this book
   so that you will remember what you want to talk about.

Choose an Unforgettable Tip and a Post-Date Idea from the
lists at the end of the chapter.

**DATE IDEA #3**

## Massage Message
*(Rating: flexible, easy to plan, low expense)*

Nothing can be more relaxing to a man than a massage. You
might want to do a little research about how to give a good

massage. Find a book in the library that will give you some basics. Consider what the book says about lotions or oils to use in a massage.

You can do this at any time, but it would be most romantic to be alone, to have candles lit and soft music playing. Ask your husband to lie down on the bed or the floor, and then begin your magic. Massages are not just of the back—massages go all over the head, the neck, down the arms onto the hands, and down the legs onto the feet. You don't have to be an expert masseuse in order to do this. Just a good rubdown will help your husband to relax and feel very loved.

As a final touch, you could take a bath or shower together. Then you take it from there.

You can discuss your Let's Talk questions during the massage or later in the evening.

### Prep Steps

- ○ Make sure your husband knows that a particular evening is just for you and him.
- ○ If you have children, schedule a baby-sitter who will take the kids elsewhere. You need the house to yourselves.
- ○ If you desire, go to the library and read about massage techniques so you can feel a little more comfortable.
- ○ Purchase some lotion or oil that you can use in the massage.
- ○ Light candles, put on soft music.
- ○ Select the Let's Talk questions you would like to discuss with your husband (write them down or mark them in this book). Then take along either your list or this book so that you will remember what you want to talk about.

Choose an Unforgettable Tip and a Post-Date Idea from the lists at the end of the chapter.

**DATE IDEA #4**

# Away with Him!
*(Rating: not flexible, lots of planning, expensive)*

Plan a romantic overnight getaway for the two of you. Perhaps you can reserve a night at a nice bed-and-breakfast. Or maybe a hotel with a hot tub. Do a little research, and find a place far enough away that you will feel as if you're on a mini-vacation, and you can enjoy lots of privacy. Also, look for those "romantic" things that would be a plus for your night away—a room with a fireplace, hot tub, etc.

Arrive at your husband's office, pick him up either early or directly after work, and take him to your secret location. Often it takes getting away from the distractions of the house, the telephone, and the children in order to really focus on each other.

At some point during the date, discuss your Let's Talk questions.

## Prep Steps

○ Decide on the target date. Check with your husband in noncommittal terms so that he keeps the evening and the next morning (or day!) free on his schedule.

○ Check with his boss to see about letting your husband off a couple hours early. If not, tell your husband to be ready right after work.

○ Make reservations for dinner and your overnight stay.

○ Provide for baby-sitting, if needed.

○ If you can pull it off, pack his luggage ahead of time so that the weekend away can be a complete surprise. In your baggage, pack some sexy lingerie. If you don't have any and your budget allows, indulge yourself (trust me, this is an expense your husband won't mind!).

○ Pack some treats in the car for the ride to the location you've selected.

○ Select the Let's Talk questions you would like to discuss with your husband (write them down or mark them in this book). Then take along either your list or this book so that you will remember what you want to talk about.

Choose an Unforgettable Tip and a Post-Date Idea from the lists below.

~ ~ ~

## Unforgettable Tips

1. Tell your husband what a "hunk" he is—and say it with passion. Don't be afraid to tell him what you love about him.
2. Purchase some new lingerie for your date with your husband. Or splurge on some satin sheets. Or scented candles. Anything that will enhance the sensuality of your time together.
3. Tell him that you are committed to meeting his sexual needs and that you always want to be there for him. (Many of the Let's Talk questions will guide you through a discussion of how he would like you to meet his needs.)
4. Men are wired to respond to visual stimulation. Use your imagination in the security and privacy of your date to be as stimulating as possible!

## Post-Date Ideas

1. Call your husband during the day, and tell him that he is your one and only and that you can't wait to have some special time with him!
2. Leave a few sexy notes to stir the passion (always in very discreet places where only he will find them).
3. When you notice times when he is helping to meet a need of yours (helping with dinner, cleaning, talking with you, working with the kids), whisper your apprecia-

tion in his ear and add that you can't wait to have some private time with him.

4. Relearn the art of flirting—but only with your husband, of course! Practice winking from across the room. Whatever used to work will still work now!

5. Initiate sex with your husband. Remember his needs, and be ready to be there for him! When he initiates, respond positively—no matter how tired you feel. If you absolutely cannot, be sure he understands why.

6. Put into practice at least one thing you talked about.

## Let's Talk

Choose some questions/comments from each level to help guide your discussion during your date. This way you can learn more about how you can meet your husband's need for sexual intimacy.

### LEVEL 1:
*Dip Your Toes into the Water*

- Each of you answer these questions: "How did you learn about sex when you were growing up? How was it taught to you?"
- "Do we have enough privacy for intimacy? What do we need to do to assure privacy?"
- "What would you think if I bought myself some revealing or 'creative' nightgowns or underwear?"
- "In what type of setting have you always wanted to make love?"
- "Do you ever feel anxious about making love? If so, when and why?"

### LEVEL 2:
*Up to Your Ankles*

- "How often do you want to make love?"
- "Should we attempt to 'schedule' lovemaking so that we are

assured of private time together? How can we make sure that we don't go too long without sexual intimacy?"

- "Is sex helpful, comforting, difficult, or anxiety producing for you when you are under stress? How can our intimacy at those times be at its best?"
- "Do you think that sex brings us closer, or does closeness lead to sex? Do you appreciate one more than the other?"

**LEVEL 3:**

*Treading in Deeper Waters*

- "Do you ever give me signals that mean you want to make love? Am I missing them? Should we come up with some signals that we can give to each other?"
- "What satisfies you most about our sexual relationship? What would you like to change?"
- "Do you ever wish that I would initiate sex more often? How would you like me to do it?"
- "Do you think we could be more imaginative in the area of sexual expression? What are your suggestions or ideas?" (If your husband suggests things that you are not comfortable doing, talk about your uneasiness.)
- Each of you answer these questions: "What part of my body do you find most exciting? What behavior do you find most exciting?"

**LEVEL 4:**

*Bouncing on the Waves*

- "What excites you the most about me sexually? What do you want me to do to take advantage of that?"
- "There may be times when you want sex, and I simply can't do it right then. How can I let you know that without hurting you? In what ways can I say no so that you hear, 'Not now, but definitely later'?"
- "Do you ever feel that I use sex as a reward? Have I ever withheld sex in order to punish you? When? How did you feel? What should we do so that it doesn't happen again?"

- "Do I ever act as if sex is more of a duty than a pleasure? What are some ideas on how that could change?"

**LEVEL 5:**

## Diving in Head First

- If sex has been difficult for you because of a situation in your past or a current problem, talk to your husband about this. Be honest. Consider together how best to deal with this. If professional help is needed, don't be too afraid or ashamed to say so.
- "What words or actions on my part throughout the day or week really set the stage for a great time of lovemaking?"
- Complete this sentence for your husband, "Five things you could do during the week that would 'warm me up' for sex are . . ."
- Each of you answer the following question, "I most want to make love to you when . . ."

# Chapter Twelve

# A Date to Meet My Husband's Need for Unconditional Love and Acceptance

## GARY SHARES IDEAS WITH WIVES

"Julia, I am so discouraged. The new business is not showing a profit. In fact, I think we are in jeopardy of losing it if it doesn't turn in the next ninety days. The bank called, again. I feel kind of used up, like I've lost the edge. And to top it off I have been winded recently just climbing the stairs. My exercise time is down to zilch, and those drive-through lunches are taking a toll."

"I love you no matter what, Tom. That was true the day we shared wedding cake, and it is even *more* true today. I am yours. You are mine. We are God's. Nothing will separate us from each other." Julia rubbed her husband's back as they talked. She knew he was shaken.

"I know that, Julia. At least I think I know that, but so much has happened. What are we going to do? This is not what we planned for our lives."

"Remember, honey, there is always a beginning, a middle, and an end to these tough times. I think we are in the middle of this one, but we'll get through it—together. I know our lives are being shaken, but we have to remember that God is holding the saltshaker."

Tom was heading into a full-blown crisis, and his perception of his capacity to be all he wanted to be for Julia and their kids had taken a downturn. Julia's response to him helped a lot. Her verbal expression of belief in him was important, but even more invaluable was her expression of commitment to him and her reminder that they would get through this— together.

Julia was being what Barb and I like to call "God with skin on" to Tom, and it was making a difference.

## The Number One Love Need of Men

As different as men and women are, we discovered from our survey that both men and women have the same number one love need. Both men and women desire to be loved unconditionally.

What does that mean? It means to be loved without conditions, to be loved no matter what, and to be loved even when we've messed up. Conditional love says, "I love you *if . . .*" Unconditional love says, "I love you *even if . . .*" You see the difference? Conditional love requires a person to meet certain conditions in order to be loved. Unconditional love says that even when the person doesn't meet those conditions, he or she is loved anyway.

Wives desire to be loved unconditionally by their husbands. You need to be secure in your husband's love even when you're sad or distressed, when you've failed, when you've hurt him, or when you don't feel so good about yourself. You need to know that he is there for you, still loves you, and will never leave you. Perhaps when you got married, your husband said these words, "for better or worse, for richer and for poorer, in sickness and in health, as long as we both shall live." (If you didn't say exactly that, the sentiment to whatever vows you spoke was essentially the same.) In other words, he was saying that he would always love you *unconditionally*. (Now, if that seems to be a problem, don't worry. Barb is talking to your husbands about this love need of yours in her date chapter for them.)

And most likely, at that same wedding ceremony, you said the same words back to him. In other words, you also promised to love your husband *unconditionally*. It didn't seem like such a big deal to say those words on that beautiful day with that handsome man standing in front of you. But years into the marriage—after he may have made some mistakes in his job or with finances, after he may have become distant, after he may have hurt you, after he may have faced an illness—the weight of those promises you made becomes very real.

That's when you need to take the challenge to love unconditionally.

## When the Storms Come

During times of crisis or stress in a man's life, he needs to know that his wife is going to be there for him through it all. When he feels like a failure, when he's made big mistakes, or when he's hurt you, he wonders if he will face rejection or find understanding from you. When your husband comes to you in the depths of such situations, seeking your love, will he find it? When he looks into your eyes and sees unconditional, "even if" love, he has found a treasure beyond all value. When you remind him that you are always there for him and that you will stick with him like glue through whatever storms come your way, then you are showing your husband the power of unconditional love.

And it isn't easy. After all, this kind of love, *agape* love, is the love Christ showed to us when he died on the cross. It is love without strings attached, love that loves the sinner, love that expects nothing in return, love that sacrifices for the good of another.

In other words, this kind of love comes from the heart of God. In order to have this kind of love, you need to be in touch with God's heart. The Holy Spirit gives you the ability to love this way. You don't have to try to generate it yourself—for the times when such love is most needed are the times when you will *least* feel like giving it. That's why you need to draw on God's power and grace in order to be able to give that unconditional love.

Has your unconditional love ever been put to the test? Have the vows that you took on your wedding day to love your husband in good times and bad ever been put through the crucible of painful reality? How did you react? Did you show your husband *conditional* love or *unconditional* love? Conditional love can cripple your husband and tear him apart. Unconditional love will build him up and help him to move through the problem, learn and grow, all the while drawing closer to you.

Your response and connection to your husband in those situations are crucial to the health of your marriage and family. The ability to stand with your husband even through the painful times is the foundation to a great marriage.

### A Safe Harbor

Your husband desperately needs to know that you will accept him no matter what (and isn't that what you need from him as well?). He needs you to show grace in his weakness. Forgive him. Stand with him even when he has failed. Encourage him during times of stress. Remind him that you love him. If he seems to be drifting from his moorings, be his anchor and hold on tight.

Affirm your husband as often as possible. Tell him that you are proud of him. Thank him when he does things that show his love for you. Tell him he's God's blessing to you. Be specific about things that you appreciate about him. Help your husband to feel safe. Provide a safe harbor for him in the storms of life.

Take time to connect with your husband. The first few moments at the end of the workday when you and he are together is a crucial time for your marriage. If you don't do it already, you need to set aside at least fifteen minutes to simply focus on each other. Put dinner on hold, let the kids be on their own, and talk through the mundane details of the day that each of you experienced. Listen to each other. Connect. Why? Because unconditional love can only occur in the context of communication and true connection.

Then be a student of your husband. Every man is different. In order to know how to express unconditional love to the man in your life, you need to understand his rhythms and his moods. As a result, you'll understand him better and you'll relate to him better.

When you give your husband grace, affirmation, safety, time, and study, you are giving him your unconditional love.

## Pre-Date Ideas

Before you consider the suggested dates in this section, I'd like you to think about your husband for a few minutes. Focus on the following questions:

_ Where do I need to show some grace, real grace, to the man I married? Where do I need to let go and let God do his thing with him?

_ Am I studying my husband? Do I know his strengths as well as his weaknesses?

_ What kind of stress is he under today? Do I know what he faces each day?

_ Has he hurt or failed me? How have I dealt with it?

_ How often do I affirm him?

_ Do I show him unconditional love?

Your husband is not perfect—you probably already know that. And he knows it as well. You can take your knowledge of his faults and use it against him. You can refuse to show

unconditional love until he straightens up (which is a contra-
diction). You can withhold other things from him (such as
communication or sex) until he overcomes his problems. You
can do those things—and you will damage your marriage in
the process.

Or you can choose to love unconditionally. You can look at
that man whom you married and promised to love forever and
say, "I know you better now. I see your faults much more
clearly. I've been hurt and disappointed by you. *But I still love
you, and I will always love you!"* When you do that for your
husband, you are keeping the vows you made before God and
you are giving him a priceless gift.

And you won't be sorry.

*Four Suggested Dates with Your Husband*

**DATE IDEA #1**

# Getting Cozy with Coffee
*(Rating: flexible, easy to plan, low expense)*

Go to a coffeehouse or a cozy café. Choose a place where
you're not likely to run into anyone you know (interruptions
aren't allowed). You can go for dinner, a couple of big cups of
specialty coffee, or a dessert. Splurge a little. Don't think about
calories or how much that big cup of cappuccino is costing—
just do it! Sit so that you can look at each other as you talk.
Hold hands—just don't embarrass the other patrons! This
kind of setting is made for conversation, so use the time to ask
your husband some of the Let's Talk questions.

### Prep Steps
○ Get the date on everyone's calendar.
○ Schedule a baby-sitter, if needed.
○ Decide on a location that will be cozy yet conducive to
   conversation. Make reservations if you think it's necessary.

○ Select the Let's Talk questions you would like to discuss with your husband (write them down or mark them in this book). Then take along either your list or this book so that you will remember what you want to talk about.

Choose an Unforgettable Tip and a Post-Date Idea from the lists at the end of the chapter.

**DATE IDEA #2**
# I'm on Your Side
*(Rating: very flexible, easy to prepare—you'll just need to think about how to do it best, low expense)*

Has your husband been through a tough time lately? What's been going on at work? Does your husband know that you love him no matter what? What challenges your ability to love him unconditionally?

- Has he failed at something at work, and has this affected his self-esteem?
- Has there been a betrayal, a huge disappointment, even infidelity? Perhaps this occurred in the past, but it is still affecting your marriage.
- Have you both been at odds because of the amount of time he's been away from you and focused on his job?

Your husband doesn't want to be weak or appear weak to anyone—especially you. However, you're the first person who will see and experience any weakness in his armor. How you respond to him can make the difference between helping him go on or defeating him completely.

No matter what kind of hurt you're experiencing, your husband desperately needs to know that you love him unconditionally. When you say to him, "I love you no matter what," both you and he need to know what that "what" is. You need to be able to say to him, "I love you even though your job

didn't work out," or "I love you even though you're unsure of
our future," or "I love and forgive you for past mistakes," or "I
love you even though you've been unable to be very attentive
to the family recently."

Identify a situation that needs healing or reconciliation.
Then arrange a date around that situation. You might take
your husband to the parking lot of his office—the place
where he is facing great difficulty or failure or the place that
is taking so much time away from his family because of his
job's demands. As you sit in that parking lot, tell him that
you love him "no matter what." Affirm him. If he's losing his
job, let him know that God knows the future and will take
care of your family. If there has been betrayal or infidelity
(either emotional or physical), go to a church parking lot or
a chapel and speak words of recommitment and healing to
him.

Show grace in his weakness. Be his anchor. Help him feel
safe with you. Assure him that you are committed and will
work through the situation with him.

Take the time to talk through your Let's Talk questions.
Pray together about the situation. Your desire for this date is
that your husband will know beyond a doubt that you love
him "no matter what." This security will help him to face
the situation head on, knowing of your full support and
love.

### Prep Steps

○ Get the date on everyone's calendar.

○ Schedule a baby-sitter, if needed.

○ Think about where you want to go. What location will
be most meaningful so that your husband understands
the connection? What location will allow for conversation alone together to talk through the issue at
hand?

○ Select the Let's Talk questions you would like to discuss

with your husband (write them down or mark them in this book). Then take along either your list or this book so that you will remember what you want to talk about.

Choose an Unforgettable Tip and a Post-Date Idea from the lists at the end of the chapter.

**DATE IDEA #3**

# What Memories Are Made Of
*(Rating: flexible, fairly easy [be creative], low expense)*

As a surprise, take your husband to a place of really good memories for him. Perhaps it's the local football field where you saw him play many times when he was in high school. Perhaps it's the location of your first date. What place near your home holds positive memories for your husband? Or where have you had fun together?

Go to this location. Talk about the memories. Take some time to think about the past—good or bad. Then look into the future—together. Are the memories you're making now going to be ones that you will look back on fondly? If not, how can you improve today so that it is a good memory tomorrow? Consider your Let's Talk questions.

### Prep Steps
○ Consider a location that has good memories either for your husband or for the two of you together.
○ Get this date on both of your calendars.
○ Schedule a baby-sitter, if needed.
○ Select the Let's Talk questions you would like to discuss with your husband (write them down or mark them in this book). Then take along either your list or this book so that you will remember what you want to talk about.

Choose an Unforgettable Tip and a Post-Date Idea from the lists at the end of the chapter.

**DATE IDEA #4**

## Let's Dream!
*(Rating: probably not very flexible, will take research and planning, may be expensive)*

This idea is a bit extravagant. You're going to plan something over and above anything you might normally consider for a date. This is going to be your opportunity to make one of your husband's dreams come true. As you've studied your husband and truly listened to him, you should have some clues as to some things he has always wanted to do. You're going to try to make this happen for him.

Maybe he's always wanted to go to a World Series or Super Bowl game. Perhaps he's always wanted to take one of those one-day skydiving classes. Maybe he's always wanted to visit the New York Stock Exchange. Perhaps he's wanted to go hunting, golfing, or fishing in a particular location.

Think back, and see if you can remember something your husband has said he has always wanted to do—or just ask him. Of course, there may be some money issues to work out, but let your husband know that you want to do something extra special for him, something to show that you love him so much you want to make one of his dreams come true. Unconditional love is love that gives—and what better way to give than to make your husband's dream come true and to join him in his dream! Join him if that would enhance the experience, and I think for most men it would. It would show him that you are sacrificing to meet a deep need in him and that you desire to enter his world. When we as men have these dreams, we often think to ourselves, *I'll never experience it.* Or, *With all the needs our family has, how could I rationalize the expense?* As a result, we may never really pursue them. When you step out of your own need to focus on fulfilling a dream for your husband, he feels a hundred feet tall.

When you've hit upon an idea, make the appropriate plans.

*Gary Talks to Wives*

Getting two tickets for the World Series may be a challenge and takes perfect timing (is his favorite team going to be there, or does it matter?). But if you can pull it off, it will be well worth the effort. A skydiving class can be arranged with a few phone calls (and okay, he may be fine with you watching from the ground!). Other excursions can be planned so that the two of you can enjoy a very special time living his dream and making memories you'll both cherish forever.

After the date, set aside some time to do your Let's Talk questions.

### Prep Steps

- ○ Get the date for your date on everyone's schedule.
- ○ Schedule a baby-sitter, if needed.
- ○ Tell your husband how to dress for this particular outing.
- ○ Make the required reservations.
- ○ Buy some fun kind of clue to leave for him on the day of the date. If he's going skydiving, buy one of those toy parachutes and tape it to the bathroom mirror.
- ○ Select the Let's Talk questions you would like to discuss with your husband (write them down or mark them in this book). Then take along either your list or this book so that you will remember what you want to talk about.

Choose an Unforgettable Tip and a Post-Date Idea from the lists below.

~ ~ ~

### *Unforgettable Tips*

1. At some time during the date, look your husband in the eyes and say, "I love you no matter what. I am here for you no matter what."

2. If your husband is a reader, what is his favorite book? Purchase a copy of it as a gift for him. Tell him that choosing a favorite book is like a marriage. When you are choosing a book, you look at the cover first. Tell him you

like his "cover" very much, even if it is getting a little "ragged" over time! But a book becomes a true favorite after it has been read cover to cover. Tell him that you know him deep inside, even with all the flaws, and you love him anyway. He is your favorite because you know more than the cover, you know him deep within. But unlike a book that can be read once and put aside, you want to continue to read and learn more every day for the rest of your life.

3. Purchase a flashlight—perhaps a nice big one or a tiny key chain flashlight. Tell him that this is a reminder that you want to "connect" with him daily and that the "connection" is what makes for the "light" in your marriage. The flashlight is meant to be a constant reminder of your desire to connect with him and of the fact that he is the light of your life.

### Post-Date Ideas

1. Every day for the next week or so, leave him a note or tell him, "I want you to know that I really appreciate you because . . ."
2. Set aside a few minutes every day to connect with each other. This may be those first few minutes when you both are at home together. Allow time for a few minutes for each of you to talk about your day. Be undistracted so you can listen to each other.
3. Begin to work on at least one item you talked about during your discussion questions.

### Let's Talk

Choose some questions/comments from each level to help guide your discussion during your date. This way you can learn more about how you can meet your husband's need for unconditional love.

**LEVEL 1:**

## Dip Your Toes into the Water

- "Are we making time to connect with each other daily? How should we improve that?"
- "What was your day like today? What are the stresses you have been feeling in the past few months?"
- "What does the term *unconditional love* mean to you? How do/can you know that I love you unconditionally? What can I do better?"
- "When was the last time we went deeper with each other? How did you feel? What can I do to make it more comfortable?"

**LEVEL 2:**

## Up to Your Ankles

- "What burdens (emotional, financial, spiritual) do we have now that we didn't have ten years ago? five years ago? last year? How can we adjust to them together?"
- Make a list of five things that you have always been able to count on your husband for, read that list to him, and thank him.
- Finish this statement to your husband, "I am proud of you because . . ."
- "Do I affirm you enough? What can I do better so that you know how much I appreciate and love you?"

**LEVEL 3:**

## Treading in Deeper Waters

- "What are we doing to build safety into our marriage so we can take the risks to love unconditionally?"
- "Do you ever sense that I sometimes put conditions on my love for you? If so, what are the conditions that you feel I am placing on you? When do you feel the most insecure about my love?"
- Tell your husband at least five areas where your love for him has deepened since you've been married.

- "Am I a safe haven for you? In what ways can I make you feel safer sharing your thoughts with me?"

**LEVEL 4:**

*Bouncing on the Waves*

- Ask your husband to complete one or more of the following questions/sentences:
    1. "Would you love me even if I . . . ?"
    2. "I need your love especially when I . . ."
    3. "I sometimes feel that I don't deserve your love because . . ."
    4. "You would never love me if you knew . . ."

    Respond to his statement with loving words that make him feel secure in your love.
- "What three things do I do for you that really make you feel like the man of my dreams? What would you like me to do?"
- "What in any way makes you doubt that my love for you is growing deeper, expanding wider, and becoming more real than it was last year?"
- "When I need to confront you about something, how should I go about it? How do you feel when I point out an area in your life that I think needs some growth? When should I speak up?"

**LEVEL 5:**

*Diving in Head First*

- "Have I ever broken your heart? If so, when? How could I have handled that situation differently? What can I do to heal that situation?"
- If your husband has been unfaithful to you (either emotionally or physically), say, "I want you to know that I forgive you for [whatever the circumstances were]. I'm sorry that I contributed to that situation by [whatever you feel was your part]. How can I help you feel so secure in

my love that you will never look beyond our marriage for satisfaction?"

- If you have ever been unfaithful to your husband (and he knows about it), say, "I am sorry that I violated our relationship. I ask you to forgive me again. I want to commit myself to becoming the wife you need me to be by learning to meet your needs. What is the next step you need me to take?"
- "Where do I need to show you more grace? Where do I need to let go and let God do his work in you?"

# *Part Four*

# So Keep It Up!

# Chapter Thirteen

# Make a *Good* Marriage
# a *Great* Marriage

No matter how you would currently characterize your marriage ("good," "could improve," or "we really need help"), your marriage can indeed be great! While many factors go into making a great marriage, beginning to work on your spouse's love needs is a perfect place to begin.

It is important for you to recognize, however, that you need to give yourself and your spouse some time. If you have been having difficulty for a while, recognize that you didn't get there overnight and you won't resolve everything overnight. But you can begin today to work on reconnecting, rekindling the flame, and reuniting your hearts and souls. So get a correct perspective on your situation.

You know that whenever you read an advertisement for a new diet or exercise program, it always includes the caveat that you should "check with your doctor before starting." Well, as you begin this process of strengthening your marriage, check with the Doctor first—that is, reconnect with God and be in prayer. You don't need to see *if* you should work on your marriage—that's already a given. But seek God's help for wisdom and discernment as you consider *how* to go about it. If there has been much pain and hurt in your marriage, you may need extra strength and courage to forgive or to ask for forgiveness. Take a look at my (Gary's) book, *Dr. Rosberg's Do-It-Yourself Relationship Mender* (Tyndale House and Focus on the Family) for a proven process of closing the loop and experiencing and granting forgiveness in your relationship. If there has been distance, you need wisdom to know how to reconnect. Ask God to bless your endeavor. Ask him to help you and your spouse as you work on making your marriage a *great* marriage.

In addition to prayer and perspective, you need to make a commitment. You need to "do" the dates, but not just as a quick fix you hope will make your spouse happy that his or her love need has been "met." These dates are only a start. That's why we've included the Post-Date Ideas in each section. You need to maintain your marriage by constantly being aware of your spouse's love needs. The dates include Let's Talk questions that we hope provide lots of information for you to process and use as you seek to continue to meet your spouse's love needs in the ways that will be most meaningful.

In short, keep it up! Don't stop dating just because you did one for each need or because you've done all four and have run out of ideas. Be creative! Your dates don't have to be expensive or elaborate, they just need to *be*. You and your spouse need special times together. If you have children, you need time alone. If you are empty nesters and already alone together, then you need time doing special things together. That's what dating is all about. It should never stop!

So keep on dating!

### Extra, Bonus Ideas

Here are a few dates that aren't so much focused on one or the other as on both of you.

#### We Belong Together
Here's a date where you both can make a recommitment to each other. Plan to go out for dinner. Beforehand, each of you

should draw up a list titled, "Here's What Is Special in Our Marriage." Share those lists at dinner. Celebrate all that you've done together, all that you've accomplished, all that you've weathered, and all that makes you unique. Take joy in your future together.

### Remember Those Vows

Surely you'll find yourselves invited to a wedding at some point. Take that invitation as an opportunity for a date. This can be a time to remember your own wedding. Listen carefully to the pastor's words to the married couple—listen as if the words were being spoken to you. Then listen carefully once again to the vows. Remember that these are the words you spoke to each other. Take time after the wedding to discuss ways that you have kept those vows and ways that you need to improve. Maybe even go home and pull out your own wedding video (or, if you are our vintage, the cassette tape). Revisit your wedding and the feelings and goals you had then. Reflect on God's goodness to you in the intervening years.

### Growing Together

If you have an opportunity to attend some kind of marriage enrichment conference, go ahead and go together. Take the chance to learn a bit more about your marriage, to learn more about each other, and to grow together emotionally and spiritually. Join Barb and me at one of our America's Family Coaches conferences (for scheduling, see our Web site: www.afclive.com), or experience a "weekend to remember" at a FamilyLife Conference (for scheduling, see the Web site: www.familylife.com). If our radio program *America's Family Coaches LIVE* is on in your city, then each day try to listen and do what many of our listeners tell us they do: talk about our radio program over dinner and share new ideas and insights on how to strengthen your own marriage and family.

### Take Every Opportunity

Take advantage of any moments you can grab to be together. Is he running to the video store to return the tape? Then go along for the ride. Is she going to the corner store to pick up milk? Go along. Even a few minutes grabbed from the regular rush of life can add up to a lot of time to be together.

### Together in the Quiet

The flip side of the "Take Every Opportunity" date is this one. Sometimes we need quiet time. Sometimes we need to know the other person is there, but we're in the middle of processing something or devouring a great novel or doing some paperwork. A date can consist of two people together doing different things. Don't be afraid to give each other some space.

### Make the Mundane Special

Do you both need to attend a political fund-raising dinner? Do you need to go to the quarterly business meeting at church? Maybe you need to renew your driver's licenses. Anything can be an opportunity for a date. You see, do the thing that has to be done, and then add a little twist. After the meeting, go out for coffee at your favorite place. After you stand in line at the driver's license facility, go get some ice cream. Anything can be the opportunity for a date if you know how to be creative.

You could make even chore time at home special—if you're *really* creative. However, it might be counterproductive for some of you to attempt to make a date out of hanging wallpaper together, so don't try to overdo this one!

### Working It Out

If you have a joint health-club membership, turn that into a date once in a while. Use the health club as a place for a tennis date or a walking date (on side-by-side machines of course) or a swimming date.

## In Closing

On our daily radio program, *America's Family Coaches LIVE,* we often take listeners' phone calls about their great date ideas. On a recent broadcast, a couple of listeners gave us some great advice.

One young woman called in and told us that her advice was to K-I-S-S. Now, she didn't mean "kiss," although we certainly have nothing against that! Instead, it was an acronym for Keep It So Simple. In other words, you don't need a lot of money or time to have a great date. It can be very simple and yet very meaningful and memorable.

A man calling from a cell phone in his truck told us that his philosophy of dating is to "seize the moment." We like that! Take advantage of the opportunity *today.* You don't know what tomorrow will bring. Don't wait to begin to work on making a great marriage.

# appendix

## Results of Love Needs Survey

The findings here represent the categorical data that emerged from our survey of 700 couples in 8 cities. We gave each husband and each wife a list of 20 needs and asked them to rank them in order of importance. The lists here represent their choices.

How would you have ranked the needs? How would your spouse have ranked the needs?

### Husbands' Needs

1. Unconditional love and acceptance
2. Sexual Intimacy
3. Companionship
4. Encouragement and affirmation
5. Spiritual intimacy
6. Trust
7. Honesty and openness
8. Communication and emotional intimacy
9. Family relationships
10. To be desired
11. Career support
12. To provide and protect
13. Personal time

### Wives' Needs

1. Unconditional love and acceptance
2. Emotional intimacy and communication
3. Spiritual intimacy
4. Encouragement and affirmation
5. Companionship
6. Family relationships
7. Honesty and openness
8. Nonsexual touch
9. Security and stability
10. Romance
11. Trust
12. Understanding and empathy
13. Sexual intimacy

14. Understanding and empathy

14. Personal time

15. Admiration

15. To be desired

16. Security and stability

16. Domestic support

17. Significance

17. To provide and protect

18. Romance

18. Significance

19. Domestic support

19. Admiration

20. Nonsexual touch

20. Career support

# about the authors

**Dr. Gary and Barbara Rosberg** are America's Family Coaches—equipping and encouraging America's families to live and finish life well. Having been married since 1975, Gary and Barbara have a unique message for couples. Their best-selling *The Five Love Needs of Men and Women,* a Gold Medallion finalist, is having an impact on marriages across the country.

As a result of the Rosbergs' passion for divorce-proofing America's families—for the sake of the next generation—they soon will launch a nationwide campaign to equip groups of couples to divorce-proof their marriages as well as the marriages of people in their families, churches, and neighborhoods. *Divorce-Proof Your Marriage,* the cornerstone book in that campaign, helps couples understand the vulnerable spots in their marrige and work toward loving in ways that prevent distance, discord, and emotional divorce.

Together Gary and Barbara host a nationally syndicated, daily radio program, *America's Family Coaches . . . LIVE!* On this live call-in program heard in cities all across the country, they coach callers on many family-related issues. Gary and Barbara also host a Saturday radio program on the award-winning secular WHO Radio.

**Gary,** who earned his Ed.D. at Drake University, has been a marriage and family counselor for twenty years. He has written two best-selling books: *Dr. Rosberg's Do-It-Yourself Relationship Mender* and *Guard Your Heart.* Gary coaches CrossTrainers, a men's Bible study and accountability group of more than six hundred men.

**Barbara** joined Gary in writing a special chapter for *Guard Your Heart* and in writing a study titled *Improving Communication in Your Marriage* (Group Publishing) for FamilyLife HomeBuilders Couple Series. In addition to speaking to families, Barbara speaks to women, coaching and encouraging them by emphasizing their incredible value and worth in countless roles.

The Rosbergs live outside Des Moines, Iowa, and are the parents of two adult daughters, Sarah and Missy, and the grandparents of three grandchildren.

For more information on the ministries
of America's Family Coaches,
contact:

America's Family Coaches
2540 106th Street, Suite 101
Des Moines, Iowa 50322
1-888-ROSBERG
www.afclive.com

### *Tune in to* America's Family Coaches . . . LIVE!

Listen every weekday for strong coaching on all your marriage, family, and relationship questions. On this interactive, call-in broadcast, Gary and Barbara Rosberg tackle real-life issues by coaching callers on many of today's hottest topics. Tune in, and be encouraged by America's leading family coaches.

For a listing of radio stations broadcasting *America's Family Coaches . . . LIVE,* call 1.888.ROSBERG or visit our Web site at www.afclive.com.